The Scarlet Letter

By Nathaniel Hawthorne

Literature Guide Developed by Rosemary Stassi
for *Secondary Solutions*®

ISBN-10: 0-9789204-5-7
ISBN-13: 978-0-9789204-5-6

Secondary Solutions.
THE *FIRST* SOLUTION FOR THE SECONDARY TEACHER®
WWW.4SECONDARYSOLUTIONS.COM

The Scarlet Letter
Complete Literature Guide

About This Literature Guide

Secondary Solutions is the endeavor of a high school English teacher who could not seem to find appropriate materials to help her students master the necessary concepts at the secondary level. She grew tired of spending countless hours researching, creating, writing, and revising lesson plans, worksheets, quizzes, tests and extension activities to motivate and inspire her students, and at the same time, address those ominous content standards! Materials that were available were either juvenile in nature, skimpy in content, or were moderately engaging activities that did not come close to meeting the content standards on which her students were being tested. Frustrated and tired of trying to get by with inappropriate, inane lessons, she finally decided that if the right materials were going to be available to her and other teachers, she was going to have to make them herself! Mrs. Bowers set to work to create one of the most comprehensive and innovative Literature Guide sets on the market. Joined by a middle school teacher with 21 years of secondary school experience, **Secondary Solutions** began, and has since matured into a specialized team of intermediate and secondary teachers who have developed for you a set of materials unsurpassed by all others.

Before the innovation of **Secondary Solutions**, materials that could be purchased offered a reproducible student workbook and a separate set of teacher materials at an additional cost. Other units provided the teacher with student materials only, and very often, the content standards were ignored. **Secondary Solutions** provides all of the necessary materials for complete coverage of the literature units of study, including author biographies, pre-reading activities, numerous and varied vocabulary and comprehension activities, study-guide questions, graphic organizers, literary analysis and critical thinking activities, essay-writing ideas, extension activities, quizzes, unit tests, alternative assessment, and much, much more. Each Guide is designed to address the unique learning styles and comprehension levels of every student in your classroom. All materials are written and presented at the grade level of the learner, and include *extensive coverage of the content standards*. As an added bonus, all teacher materials are *included*!

As a busy teacher, you don't have time to waste reinventing the wheel. You want to get down to the business of *teaching*! With our professionally developed teacher-written Literature Guides, **Secondary Solutions** has provided you with the answer to your time management problems while saving you hours of tedious and exhausting work. Our Guides will allow you to focus on the most important aspects of teaching—the personal, one-on-one, hands-on instruction you enjoy most—the reason you became a teacher in the first place.

Secondary Solutions®
The *First* Solution for the Secondary Teacher®
www.4secondarysolutions.com

How to Use Our Literature Guides

Our Literature Guides are based upon the *National Council of the Teachers of English* and the *International Readers Association's* national English/Language Arts Curriculum and Content Area Standards. The materials we offer allow you to teach the love and full enjoyment of literature, while still addressing the concepts upon which your students are assessed.

These Guides are designed to be used in their sequential entirety, or may be divided into separate parts. Not all activities must be used, but to achieve full comprehension and mastery of the skills involved, it is recommended that you utilize everything each Guide has to offer. Most importantly, you now have a variety of valuable materials to choose from, and you are not forced into extra work!

There are several distinct categories within each Literature Guide:

- *Exploring Expository Writing*—Worksheets designed to address the exploration and analysis of functional and/or informational materials. For example:
  - ✓ *Author Biography*
  - ✓ *Biographies of non-fiction characters*
  - ✓ *Relevant news and magazine articles, etc.*
  - ✓ *Articles on historical context*
- *Comprehension Check*—Similar to *Exploring Expository Writing*, but designed for comprehension of narrative text—study questions designed to guide students *as they read the text.*
- *Standards Focus*—Worksheets and activities that directly address the content standards and allow students extensive practice in literary skills and analysis. *Standards Focus* activities are found within every chapter or section. Some examples:
  - ✓ *Figurative Language*
  - ✓ *Irony*
  - ✓ *Flashback*
- *Assessment Preparation*—Vocabulary activities which emulate the types of vocabulary/ grammar proficiency on which students are tested in state and national assessments. *Assessment Preparation* activities are found within every chapter or section. Some examples:
  - ✓ *Context Clues*
  - ✓ *Connotation/Denotation*
  - ✓ *Word Roots*
- *Quizzes and Tests*—Quizzes are included for each chapter or designated section; final tests as well as alternative assessment are available at the end of each Guide. These include:
  - ✓ *Multiple Choice*
  - ✓ *Matching*
  - ✓ *Short Response*
- *Pre-Reading, Post-Reading Activities, Essay/Writing Ideas* <u>plus</u> *Sample Rubrics*—Each Guide also has its own unique pre-reading, post-reading, essay/writing ideas, and alternative assessment activities.

Each Guide contains handouts and activities with varied levels of difficulty. We know that not all students are alike—nor are all teachers. We hope you can effectively utilize every aspect our Literature Guides have to offer—we want to make things easier on you! If you need additional assistance, please email us at info@4secondarysolutions.com. For specific information on how our Guides are directly correlated to your state's content standards, please send us an email, including the name of your state, to: contentstandards@4secondarysolutions.com. Thank you for choosing Secondary Solutions®.

Sample Agenda

Our Literature Guides are designed to be used in their sequential entirety, or may be divided into separate parts. Not all activities must be used, but to achieve full comprehension and mastery of the skills involved, it is recommended that you utilize everything each Guide has to offer. Below is a sample unit plan integrating all aspects of this *The Scarlet Letter Literature Guide*. This agenda assumes students have the time to read together as a class. It will need to be modified if you intend to have your students read on their own at home or have them complete a combination of reading in class and at home.

Week One: Introduction
Day 1: Start by asking students what they have heard or what they know or think this story might be about. Have a discussion about the themes and style of *The Scarlet Letter* so that they are prepared when they turn to the first page. To help with this, use pages 8, 9 and 16 to introduce the elements of the novel as well as some of the archaic language of the text. Have students complete the *History of the Novel* activity (pg. 9) in class. Discuss the differences between novels they have already read that may fall into the category of a romantic or gothic novel. Have students complete the *Author Biography* and questions (pgs. 10-11) for homework.
Day 2: Go over the *Author Biography*, moving into the historical context of the novel. Have students read and do the questions for *Historical Context* (pgs. 12-15) and have a class discussion about the Puritans and what they learned about them. Have them finish any unfinished reading/work on *Historical Context* for homework.
Day 3: Have students complete the *Prior Knowledge Assessment* activity on pgs. 23-24. Allow students to self-test without their articles on historical context at first, then use the articles for help filling in the rest of the answers. Pass out the full vocabulary list with or without definitions (your choice—pg. 22 or 111-112). Discuss the use of *Allusions and Terminology* (pgs. 17-21) to give them a reference for help with unfamiliar allusions or terms. At this time (or earlier, if you prefer) have students complete one of the pre-reading activities (pg. 104). You can introduce each day with a quote, or have students do more involved pre-reading activities.
Day 4: Discuss as a class Hawthorne's style and introduce *The Custom House Introductory* in the novel. Since this Introductory is quite detailed and a little more difficult to read than the rest of the novel, you may want to read this introductory in class, having students finish at home, also completing the activity (pg. 26).
Day 5: Discuss *The Custom House Introductory*, including problems, confusion, etc. Introduce the *Active Reading Guide* (pg. 25) and explain its purpose and use. Begin reading the first chapter as a class so that students hear the tone and style of the novel, and have them take notes in their *Active Reading Guide* (pg. 27) as they read. It may take a while for students to get used to the archaic language, so you may want to give them more time for the first few chapters. Have them complete the *Comprehension Check* questions for Chapter One (pg. 28) as they finish reading the chapter.

Week Two: Reading
Days 6-7: Have students continue reading Chapters 2 and 3, completing the *Active Reading Guide* (pg. 27) and *Comprehension Check* questions (pg. 28) as they read.
Day 8: Once students have finished Chapters 1-3, introduce them to *Standards Focus: Allusions* (pg. 29) and *Assessment Preparation: Definitions* (pgs. 30-31) for Chapters 1-3.
Day 9: Give *Quiz: Chapters 1-3* (pgs. 75-76). Begin reading Chapters 4-6, having students complete the new *Active Reading Guide* (pg. 32) and *Comprehension Check* questions (pg. 33) as they read.
Day 10: Have students continue reading Chapters 4-6, completing the *Active Reading Guide* (pg. 32) and *Comprehension Check* questions (pg.33) as they read.

Week Three: Reading
Day 11: Have students continue reading Chapters 4-6, completing the *Active Reading Guide* (pg. 32) and *Comprehension Check* questions (pg.33) as they read.
Day 12: Once students have finished Chapters 4-6, introduce them to *Standards Focus: Characterization* (pgs. 34-35) and *Assessment Preparation: Word Origins* (pgs. 36-37) for Chapters 4-6.
Day 13: Give *Quiz: Chapters 4-6* (pgs. 77-78). Begin reading Chapters 7-9, having students complete the new *Active Reading Guide* (pg. 38) and *Comprehension Check* questions (pg. 39) as they read.
Days 14-15: Have students continue reading Chapters 7-9, completing the *Active Reading Guide* (pg. 38) and *Comprehension Check* questions (pg. 39) as they read.

Week Four: Reading

Day 16: Once students have finished Chapters 7-9, introduce them to *Standards Focus: Conflict* (pgs. 40-42) and *Assessment Preparation: Word Parts* (pgs. 43-44) for Chapters 7-9.

Day 17: Give *Quiz: Chapters 7-9* (pgs. 79-80). Begin reading Chapters 10-12, having students complete the new *Active Reading Guide* (pg. 45) and *Comprehension Check* questions (pg. 46) as they read.

Days 18-19: Have students continue reading Chapters 10-12, completing the *Active Reading Guide* (pg. 45) and *Comprehension Check* questions (pg. 46) as they read.

Day 20: Once students have finished Chapters 10-12, introduce them to *Standards Focus: Motif* (pg. 47) and *Assessment Preparation: Connotation and Denotation* (pgs. 48-50) for Chapters 10-12.

Week Five: Reading

Day 21: Give *Quiz: Chapters 10-12* (pgs. 81-82). Begin reading Chapters 13-15, having students complete the new *Active Reading Guide* (pg. 51) and *Comprehension Check* questions (pg. 52) as they read.

Days 22-23: Have students continue reading Chapters 13-15, completing the *Active Reading Guide* (pg. 51) and *Comprehension Check* questions (pg. 52) as they read.

Day 24: Once students have finished Chapters 13-15, introduce them to *Standards Focus: Setting* (pgs. 53-54) and *Assessment Preparation: Definitions* (pgs. 55-56) for Chapters 13-15.

Day 25: Give *Quiz: Chapters 13-15* (pgs. 83-84). Begin reading Chapters 16-18, having students complete the new *Active Reading Guide* (pg. 57) and *Comprehension Check* questions (pg. 58) as they read.

Week Six: Reading

Day 26: Have students continue reading Chapters 16-18, completing the *Active Reading Guide* (pg. 57) and *Comprehension Check* questions (pg. 58) as they read.

Day 27: Once students have finished Chapters 16-18, introduce them to *Standards Focus: Symbolism* (pgs. 59-60) and *Assessment Preparation: Word Origins* (pgs. 61-62) for Chapters 16-18.

Day 28: Give *Quiz: Chapters 16-18* (pgs. 85-86). Begin reading Chapters 19-21, having students complete the new *Active Reading Guide* (pg. 63) and *Comprehension Check* questions (pg. 64) as they read.

Days 29-30: Have students continue reading Chapters 19-21, completing the *Active Reading Guide* (pg. 63) and *Comprehension Check* questions (pg. 64) as they read.

Week Seven: Reading

Day 31: Once students have finished Chapters 19-21, introduce them to *Standards Focus: Plot* (pgs. 65-66) and *Assessment Preparation: Word Parts* (pgs. 67-68) for Chapters 19-21.

Day 32: Give *Quiz: Chapters 19-21* (pg. 87). Begin reading Chapters 22-24, having students complete the new *Active Reading Guide* (pg. 69) and *Comprehension Check* questions (pg. 70) as they read.

Days 33-34: Have students continue reading Chapters 22-24, completing the *Active Reading Guide* (pg. 69) and *Comprehension Check* questions (pg. 70) as they read.

Day 35: Once students have finished Chapters 22-24, introduce them to *Standards Focus: Theme* (pg. 71) and *Assessment Preparation: Connotation and Denotation* (pgs. 72-74) for Chapters 22-24.

Week Eight: Conclusion

Day 36: Give *Quiz: Chapters 22-24* (pg. 88-89). Now that you have finished the entire novel you can start reviewing for the final exam. Take this time to let the students ask any questions about any of the worksheets or any notes they took. Use the rest of the day to talk about anything and everything in the novel so that they feel prepared for the test.

Day 37: Give either version of the exam and/or allow the students to write an essay or complete the section with any of the activities from the *Post-Reading Activities* (pg. 105) or *Essay and Writing Ideas* (pg. 106).

Day 38: Assign students any of the *Post-Reading Activities* or *Essay/Writing Ideas* so that they can come full circle in their understanding of *The Scarlet Letter*. It is helpful to create a list of teacher-approved projects/writing assignments and let your students choose the project or writing assignment that best suits their individual style or skill level. Rubrics can be found on pages 107-110.

Days 39-40: If the students are working on projects or in groups, give them one or two days of class time to work together. Allow the students to present their projects in front of the entire class and then proudly display the projects in your classroom.

Standards Focus: Important Elements of Novels

Allusion: an implied or indirect reference to a person, event, or a part of another text; not a direct quote.

> Ex. Martin Luther King Jr. started his "I Have a Dream" speech by saying "Five score years ago," which alludes to Abraham Lincoln's *Gettysburg Address* in which Lincoln said "For score and seven years ago…"

Characterization: the process of developing a three dimensional and believable representation of a character in fiction or drama; the process of making a character seem real

> Ex. Edmond Dantès's desire for revenge in *The Count of Monte Cristo* by Alexandre Dumas.

Conflict: the opposition of persons or forces upon which dramatic action depends; includes three main types: man vs. man, man vs. self, man vs. nature

> Ex. a sword fight between two characters is *man vs. man*; a character struggling with a decision is *man vs. self*; a man lost in the woods is *man vs. nature*

Foreshadowing: when an event in a story is referred to before the event actually takes place; meant to be a clue for the reader so that they can guess what may happen later in the story

> Ex. one character makes a reference to another character's possible death, and later in the story, that character dies

In Medias Res: in or into the middle of the narrative plot without the formality of an introduction or lengthy exposition; the story starts in the middle of the action

> Ex. *The Illiad* begins in the middle of the fight between Achilles and Agamemnon

Motif: a recurring thematic element which has symbolic significance in the story

> Ex. the recurrence of the green light in *The Great Gatsby*

Plot: the main story or plan of a literary work; the order of events

> Ex. the novel *Rebecca* is very plot-driven, full of mystery and romance, as the reader learns what causes Rebecca's death

Setting: the location and time frame in which the action of a narrative takes place

> Ex. the South during the Great Depression in *To Kill a Mockingbird*

Symbolism: a character or image that stands in the place of something that is often abstract or intangible; a symbol takes the place of a more obvious object, often deepening the meaning and significance in a piece of literature

> Ex. the lion is a symbol of courage; a cross is a symbol of Christianity

Theme: the dominant message or idea of a work of literature

> Ex. the loss of innocence; excessive pride can lead to ruin; what goes around, comes around

Standards Focus: The Novel—A Brief History

The long history of the novel actually starts in medieval times, when stories such as *Sir Gawain and the Green Knight* were told. These stories were called *romances* because they were often about chivalric love and knightly actions. Writers such as Chaucer, Cervantes, and Machiavelli transformed these romances into what is thought of today as the early novel format. During this time, the format of the novel was debated for many years because guidelines varied between cultures. The novel was eventually defined as a story that included any number of exciting or surprising events. *Don Quixote* by Miguel de Cervantes, is considered by many to be the first true European novel.

In the early 19th century, the novel found its first home in England, where the surge of fiction writing made novels a popular genre of literature. In 1719, Daniel Defoe wrote *Robinson Crusoe,* which opened the door to wider interpretations of the novel that would be more fully explored in early 19th century England. Increased literacy rates and the ability to mass produce literature in the 19th century allowed wider audiences access to novels. It was at this time that *The Scarlet Letter* was published in the United States. Hawthorne's international contemporaries included Charles Dickens, Emile Zola, and Fyodor Dostoyevsky.

The Gothic and Romantic Novel
After the novel became an accepted genre, a certain level of expectation fell upon someone who considered his or her piece of work a novel. Those who considered themselves novelists adhered to a set of guidelines that would eventually define the genre today. According to Webster's *Encyclopedia of Literature*, a novel is defined as a *fictional prose narrative of considerable length and a certain complexity that deals with human experience through a connected sequence of events involving a group of persons in a specific setting*. However, in no way did this mean that the novel finally adopted a uniform style/genre. For example, a novel such as *The Scarlet Letter* falls somewhere between two styles of novel writing, gothic and romantic, because Hawthorne used elements of both styles in his novel.

A traditional gothic novel, also known as the European Romantic novel, was expected to include dark and tempestuous settings full of ghosts, superstition, revenge, and madness. The gothic novel was often set in primitive medieval buildings with hidden passages and an underlying tone of terror and mystery.

On the other hand, a romantic novel was based on the ideals of chivalric love and heroic knights. Although it too evolved over time, the major components of a romantic novel include a focus on the beauty of nature, the growth of an individual's physical and emotional strength, elements of relationships and love, and the idea that insight and experience are more important than logic and science.

Comprehension Check: Novel History and Elements of the Novel
Directions: On a separate piece of paper, complete the following in complete sentences.

1. What two major factors contributed to the rise of the modern novel?
2. Why was the first form of a novel called a romance?
3. How did the definition of a novel change throughout history?
4. Do some research and find at least 2 other novels that fall into the gothic style and 2 novels that are in the romantic style.
5. From your own reading experience, choose an example for each of the novel elements on page 8. Be sure to give the story or novel's title and fully explain why this particular story or novel is a good example for the element.

Name _____ Period_____

Exploring Expository Writing: Author Biography
Nathaniel Hawthorne (1804-1864)

One of the most famous and respected authors of the Romantic Movement, Nathaniel Hawthorne was among the first writers who explored and wrote about the hidden motivations and psychology of his characters. While he did use some aspects of his own life in his novels and short stories, most of his work is remembered as a revealing look at early American history. The portrayal of Puritan and early American society in Hawthorne's novels forever changed the legacy of American literature.

Nathaniel Hawthorne (born Hathorne) was born in Salem, Massachusetts July 4, 1804. His father, Nathaniel Sr., a Captain for the U.S. Navy, died when Hawthorne was only four years old. Hawthorne's ancestors were some of the first people to settle in "The New World." John Hathorne, Hawthorne's great-grandfather, was a judge in Salem in 1692 during the Salem Witch Trials. Many scholars speculate that after having learned of his dark and scandalous family history, Hawthorne changed the spelling of his last name to include a "w."

Hawthorne attended Bowdoin College from 1821 to 1824, were he met contemporaries such as writer Henry Wadsworth Longfellow and future president Franklin Pierce. After graduating, Hawthorne became somewhat of a recluse, hiding away in his home while writing *Fanshawe* (1828) and *Twice-Told Tales* (1837). After spending many years of his life perfecting his writing, Hawthorne found a job at the Salem Custom House as port surveyor, to make ends meet. He also temporarily joined the Transcendentalist movement in 1841, and lived at Brook Farm, a utopian farming community. After less than a year of farming, Hawthorne grew tired of Brook Farm and left. His time at Brook Farm was the inspiration for his novel, *The Blithedale Romance (1852)*.

On July 9, 1842, Hawthorne married Sophia Peabody, a painter and fellow Transcendentalist. The new couple looked for a home in Concord, Massachusetts and eventually moved into The Old Manse, one of Ralph Waldo Emerson's family homes. However, due to mounting debt and other financial difficulties, the family was forced to move back to Salem, where Hawthorne once again worked at the Custom House to support his writing and his growing family. Over the years, Hawthorne and Sophia had three children, Una (1844), Julian (1846), and Rose (1851). Una, who died at a young age, was the inspiration for Pearl in *The Scarlet Letter* (1850).

After publishing *The Scarlet Letter*, Hawthorne and his family moved to Lenox, Massachusetts, where he became friends with Herman Melville. Melville saw the value and quality of Hawthorne's writing, and later dedicated his masterpiece, *Moby Dick,* to the "genius of Nathaniel Hawthorne." Hawthorne then returned to Concord, where he bought The Hillside, the former home of Louisa May Alcott's family, and renamed it The Wayside. The comfort and tranquility of this home would not last long, however, after newly-elected president Franklin Pierce appointed Hawthorne as U.S. Consul to Liverpool, England and the family left their home to head to Europe in 1853.

Finally, in 1859, Hawthorne and his family moved back to The Wayside, after traveling throughout France and Italy and collecting materials for his last novel, *The Marble Faun (1860)*. Hawthorne died on May 19, 1864, while visiting the White Mountains with Pierce. He is buried at Sleepy Hollow Cemetery in Concord, Massachusetts. Sophia Hawthorne dedicated the rest of her life to editing and publishing the rest of her husband's notebooks until she died in 1871.

Name _____ Period_____

Comprehension Check: Author Biography

Directions: *Based upon the article about Nathaniel Hawthorne, answer the following questions by writing the letter of the correct answer on the line provided.*

1. _____ What is Hawthorne best remembered for?
    a. exploring the hidden motivation and psychology of his characters
    b. the early American historical setting
    c. being part of the Romantic Movement
    d. all of the above

2. _____ What is the most likely reason that Hawthorne added a "w" to his original name, Hathorne?
    a. to make himself feel special
    b. to disguise himself with a pen name
    c. to detach himself from the actions and reputations of his ancestors
    d. to show that he could do whatever he wanted

3. _____ Hawthorne's time at Brook Farm inspired which of his novels?
    a. *The Marble Faun*
    b. *The Blithedale Romance*
    c. *Fanshawe*
    d. *Moby Dick*

4. _____ Where did Hawthorne work for most of his life to support his family?
    a. the Salem Custom House
    b. a book store
    c. in the military
    d. his writing always made enough money to support the family

5. _____ Which one of Hawthorne's children was the inspiration for Pearl from *The Scarlet Letter*?
    a. Una
    b. Julian
    c. Rose
    d. none of his children inspired him

6. _____ What great American writer saw the value of Hawthorne's writing and dedicated a major work to him?
    a. Henry Wadsworth Longfellow
    b. Franklin Pierce
    c. Ralph Waldo Emerson
    d. Herman Melville

7. On the back of this sheet or on a separate piece of paper, write a short paragraph about how Hawthorne's ancestors influenced Hawthorne's writing of *The Scarlet Letter.*

Name _____ Period_____

Standards Focus: Historical Context
Puritanism

The term *Puritan* was first used in the 1500s to refer to a religious and social movement that called for the reformation of the Church of England. The Puritans proposed that the reforms made in the Church of England during the Protestant movement be even more "purified," so that people would be governed mostly by the Laws of God, as stipulated in the Bible.

While Puritans continued to fight for how they believed their government should be run, they found that they were faced with more and more opposition during the rule of the Stuarts, King James, and King John in England. Puritans wanted to focus church services on reading the Bible, prayer, and preaching, and also believed that achieving religious virtue came from self-examination and pure devotion. Although King James did attempt to calm relations between the Puritans and the Church of England, he would not change the Church as drastically as the Puritans requested. Instead, he simply agreed to a new translation of the Bible, which is known today as the King James Version.

As the Puritans came to the realization that the Church of England was not going to meet their needs, they knew that they needed to make a dramatic change in their own lives. They had two choices: leave the Church or revolt against it. Those who revolted were led by Oliver Cromwell in 1649 in what is remembered as the English Civil War. Eventually, the Puritans gained control of government and made many unpopular changes. However, Puritan glory in England would end with the death of Cromwell, and in 1660 the Stuarts regained power. Puritan ideals did not disappear, however, and in the 1700s these ideals were revived with the rise of the Methodist Church.

Those Puritans who did not wish to engage in revolution simply left England and headed for America to begin a new life in the New World. They settled along the New England coast and shaped their lives according to their ideals: "a nation under God." Shortly after arriving, they signed the Mayflower Compact, a document which unified their hopes and dreams for the new society they were determined to establish, binding the Puritans to each other and to God. Shortly after arriving in America, they established schools and government based upon the teachings of the Bible. The schools established a standard for educational instruction, and universities like Princeton, Yale, and Harvard were established so that the proper study of Scripture would be available to the future ministers of their church. Government and religion were inescapably intertwined because the societal norms ran in conjunction with the moral codes. The Puritans also believed that government should be ruled through contracts with the people it governed, which became the bedrock of American democracy. The Puritans worked hard to build a new home in America that could support itself and withstand the test of time.

Community life in the American Puritan society was challenging because they depended only on each other and on God. Establishing their own new world in America was rough, as they had to start from the very beginning in unfamiliar territory. Often, a husband came to America first to build a home for his family; his wife and children would join him later. Towns were built so that the church was in the center of each community. The church served as a meeting hall where the men would gather to make laws, establish taxes, and assign specific tasks to members of the community. All the homes had a farm, and every member of the family who was able to work had chores to complete every day. While men caught food and did the planting, the women tended to the children, the cooking, and other chores such as making candles, clothes, and soap. Every individual depended on one another because they held firm in their belief that as a unit they could survive, but alone in the unknown wilderness, they were doomed. If one person's farm was accidentally burned, the others would help rebuild and recuperate what was lost. Life was centered upon religion, and every Sunday the entire community would gather at the church for an entire day of worship.

Standards Focus: Historical Context
Crime and Punishment in Puritan Society

Because the American Puritan society was so new and fragile, certain social expectations were placed on all citizens. Any deviation from the newly established laws and codes was seen as a form of dissention against the community as well as the rules set forth by God. In the eyes of the magistrates who ruled the Puritan society, the tight-knit community they had created could not afford to let things get out of control.

Those who committed crimes or were seen as dissenters were punished severely and publicly. Punishments centered mostly on public humiliation and the idea of vengeance. Most punishments were settled with an "eye for an eye," so if a person stole a loaf of bread, he might be branded with the letter *T* for "thief" on his hand. Most towns were required to have branding irons as a basic form of punishment. Persons who were not given the maximum punishment for their crime might be forced to stand in front of the community and confess their sins, or to wear a sign specifying their transgression, as seen in *The Scarlet Letter*.

One of the most popular forms of punishment was to be placed on the pillory, trapping the person in a large wooden stockade for a set number of hours. Often, the person would also have their ears nailed to the stockade while people threw food, trash, and anything they could get their hands on at the prisoner. But the Puritans also created far harsher punishments. A woman accused of being indecently dressed might be stripped down to her waist and whipped until her back dripped with blood. Others were dragged by their ankles all over town, pierced through the tongue, or maimed in some other way. For women who gossiped, the two most likely punishments were the ducking stool or the brank. The ducking stool was a chair attached at the end of two beams that could be extended over a river or pond so that the criminal could be dunked repeatedly into the water. The brank was a cage that fit over the head, holding the tongue by either clamping it or puncturing it so that the accused gossip could not speak.

There was only one way that a person could escape severe punishment—to declare "benefit of clergy," which was originally started so that the clergymen might have an upper hand (since they were one of the few groups that could read). "Benefit of clergy" simply meant that the accused would have to read a passage from the Bible, with no mistakes, in front of the magistrates and congregation. However, because the Bible passage was almost always the same, people started to memorize the passage and hope that they knew it well enough to please the judges into reducing their sentence or pardoning them completely.

Far worse than the fear of any punishment, however, was the underlying fear that gripped the Puritans: the fear of the devil. Because the society was so fragile and small, citizens were vulnerable and felt that they needed to take serious actions in order to defend themselves and keep their society "on the straight and narrow." Their survival rested heavily on the graciousness of God, and Puritans believed that anything that could not be explained or solved with their commonly used tools and cures was certainly the work of the devil. A sick child who could not be medically cured was said to have been seized by the devil. Dying crops were blamed on the devil. Unfortunate and circumstantial problems or issues were believed to be God's punishment or the devil at work in their community. While some people tried to find other explanations and resolutions to problems that could not be easily explained, they were often accused of conspiring with the devil and ended up being accused and often convicted of witchcraft, which was punishable by death. In Salem, the hysteria and fear of the devil became so out of hand that the Salem Witch Trials ensued and resulted in the deaths of many innocent people.

Standards Focus: Historical Context
Life as a Puritan

Because Puritan life was interdependent, the most important thing a Puritan could do was to remember his or her role as a member of the community. Puritan society was strict and anyone that challenged the everyday norms or tried to think or act only for themselves or their own family could be subject to punishment. There was a social hierarchy that was strictly respected in every community.

Most of the people who came to America to settle in the colonies came as indentured servants, and these were the people who made up the majority of the society. They were to fulfill the term of their servitude before being set free to establish a home and life for themselves. Because there was no stigma of shame associated with indentured servitude, most had no problem building homes and joining a community after being freed of their service. The other part of the community was made up of free citizens, day laborers, and day farmers—the working class. They could voice their opinions, (in a non-threatening way, of course) and be active citizens of society. However, they would always have to keep in mind those who held a higher rank.

The upper class consisted of the rich, and their presence was palpable. They enjoyed political power and respect, and indulged in the fineries of beautiful clothes and other luxuries, while always staying within the boundaries of Puritan codes. Because these aristocrats were the people who made the laws and provided order, the middle and lower class citizens were careful to ignore an aristocrat's crime or transgression. In this way, the aristocrats and clerics were held above the law.

Despite this rigid social ladder, women still had no official status in the society. Despite being seen as spiritually equal to men in the eyes of Puritan religious standards, women were subordinate to men in every way, and were expected to bow their heads to their husbands and fathers. Women could not own property, unless they were widows who had not remarried, and they had to keep their arms and hair covered. Women were hard-working and strong despite the fact that they were mostly viewed as property belonging to their husbands and gossips that constantly caused trouble. The weaker sex in this male-dominated society, women were also thought to be more susceptible to the temptation of the devil. However, there were some times when women had some influence on the way society was run, especially when a group of women gathered to express their concerns to their influential husbands.

Social Hierarchy

Upper Class—judges, preachers, and the wealthy
Middle Class—gentlemen, free citizens, and day laborers
Lower Class—indentured servants and vagabonds

Comprehension Check: Historical Context

Directions: *Use the articles on* Puritanism, Crime and Punishment in Puritan Society, *and* Life as a Puritan *to answer the questions below. Write the letter of the correct answer on the line provided.*

1. _____ What is a Puritan?
   a. A person who wants to purge himself through Baptism
   b. person who was part of the religious and social movement of the 1500s who called for the reformation of the Church of England
   c. a person who adheres strictly to the law
   d. a person who is loyal to the Church of England

2. _____ What was the name of the document that the Puritans signed upon arriving to "The New World," which bound them to each other and to God?
   a. The Magna Carta   c. The Declaration of Independence
   b. The Mayflower Compact   d. The Puritan Book of Laws

3. _____ Why were government and religion the same in the Puritan society?
   a. daily life was based on teachings from the Bible
   b. politicians and clergymen worked in conjunction to establish law and order
   c. the social norms and the religious codes both strived for the same goal—to unify a society under the laws of God
   d. all of the above

4. _____ What was in the center of town and at the center of all Puritan life?
   a. the marketplace   c. the Church and God
   b. the home of the wealthiest citizen   d. the prison

5. _____ What part of society made up the majority of the population?
   a. indentured servants   c. free citizens
   b. judges   d. clergymen

6. _____ What was the major point of the public punishments in the Puritan society?
   a. vengeance and public humiliation
   b. teaching the perpetrator how to better their life
   c. an opportunity for an impromptu sermon that the citizens had to listen to
   d. entertainment for people who were going about their daily chores

7. _____ What was the most popular form of punishment?
   a. the rack
   b. being crushed by large boulders
   c. having to stand on the pillory for hours, usually in the stockade
   d. drowning

Directions: *Using a separate piece of paper, answer the following questions using complete sentences. Be sure to support your responses with examples from the articles.*

8. Why do you think the devil was the underlying fear that terrified the citizens in Puritan society? What did the devil symbolize, aside from the obvious religious evil, in the Puritan society?

9. In a paragraph or two, explain why punishment in Puritan society was so severe. Why did Puritans take such harsh action against even the smallest crime? Why did the lawmakers and enforcers feel the need to make an example of each criminal?

10. Compare and contrast the differences in Puritan daily life and modern daily life. How have the roles of women, men, and children changed? How has the law and those who govern society changed?

Standards Focus: Historical Language

Nathanial Hawthorne published *The Scarlet Letter* in 1850, during a time when the English language was somewhat different from today. Hawthorne used terminology and dialogue that was typical of the early Puritan society, some of which is no longer in use today. Use the definitions from the list below to guide you through the less familiar language.

1. Black Man- the devil

2. canst- can

3. dost- do

4. fie- an expression of shock, like "Oh!"

5. forthwith- right away

6. gossips- women

7. hast- have; has

8. hither- here; this way

9. hold they peace- calm down; be quiet; be still

10. leech- a worm that sucks blood or eats flesh—one species has been used in medical treatments to remove bad blood or dead flesh; also, an archaic name for a doctor (who would have applied leeches for medical treatment)

11. nay- no

12. noontide- noon; 12 o'clock

13. prithee- please, I beg of you

14. Providence- God and heaven

15. savage- often refers to the Native American people and their way of life

16. skill- service

17. thither- there; that way

18. thou; thee- you

19. thy- your

20. toil- work

21. wherefore- why

Standards Focus: Allusions and Terminology

The Custom House: Introduction

1. Old Manse - the name given to the home that the grandfather of Ralph Waldo Emerson built. It was later rented by Hawthorne and his wife. Later, Hawthorne wrote *Mosses From an Old Manse* which included short stories and a description of the house.
2. "P.P. Clerk of this Parish" - refers to "Memoirs of P.P., Clerk of this Parish," which parodied the long-winded, pompous autobiography of Bishop Gilbert Burnet Hawthorne is paralleling his introduction to the literary style used in "Memoirs."
3. King Derby - Elias Hasket Derby (1739-1799), who initiated trade with the Orient from the port of Salem
4. Nova Scotia - a Canadian province located on Canada's southeastern coast; one of the first documented Scottish settlements in the Americas
5. banner of the republic…thirteen stripes turned vertically - the early American flag with 13 stars and 13 stripes
6. Uncle Sam - the national personification of the United States, popularized in the War of 1812
7. eider-down pillow - a pillow stuffed with the feathers of a sea-duck known as an Eider, found on the northern coasts of Europe and North America
8. last war with England - The American Revolutionary War with England (1775-1783)
9. mimic boats - small practice boats used for strategic planning
10. millpond - a body of water which is a result of a water-powered mill, such as a dam
11. British provinces - British-owned colonies around the world
12. Matthew - a reference to Biblical verse 9:9 in the Book of Matthew in which Jesus calls him from "the receipt of custom"
13. ship-chandler - a dealer who supplied the equipment for ships, and was also responsible for docking the ship and taking care of it while in foreign ports
14. Acts of Congress - books which contain all of the laws passed by Congress
15. Locofoco Surveyor - "Loco-foco" initially referred to the radical wing of the Democratic Party. Whigs appropriated the term from conservative Democrats and applied it negatively toward Democrats in general and toward Hawthorne in particular
16. alms-house - houses built from charitable contributions for those who are ill, elderly, widowed, or simply cannot afford housing
17. Briton – Hawthorne, a native of England, is referring to his ancestors and others from England
18. "dust for dust" - reference to Hawthorne's inextricable relationship he had with the land and with his ancestors; the saying "for dust thou art, and unto dust shalt thou return" is from *Genesis* in the Bible; essentially we started as dust and will return to dust
19. progenitor - a parent, grandparent, or other ancestor
20. Salemite - one who comes from Salem; a citizen of Salem, Massachusetts
21. sentry-march - a sentry is a guard at the entrance or gate of a location; sentry-march refers to the guards walking in formation
22. Whigs - an American political party that operated from 1834-1856
23. tide-waiters - men who worked on the docks and ports of different cities
24. "dyed in the wool" - traditional; the same way for generations
25. "born in the purple" – (*of unknown origin*); possibly born as royalty or acting like royalty
26. Revolutionary/Revolution - Revolutionary War against England (see #8)
27. fourscore - the number 80 (80 years ago)
28. Mother Nature - the personification of nature; also called Mother Earth
29. balustrade - a railing with closely spaced supports
30. Ticonderoga - a New York fort captured from the British by American forces led by Ethan Allen and Benedict Arnold
31. Chippewa - a native North American tribe
32. Fort Erie - site along the Niagara frontier where American forces won important victories in the War of 1812
33. philanthropists - charitable persons who donate much of their time, money, or talent
34. Niagara - the Native American name of a waterfall in the eastern part of the north coast of the United States
35. Providence - refers to God, fate
36. Brook Farm - the experimental Utopian society that Hawthorne and other members of the Transcendentalist movement were a part of; the community turned away from the industrialized and materialistic society that was growing around them and focused on self reliance and cooperation; the basis for Hawthorne's novel *The Blithedale Romance*
37. Emerson - Ralph Waldo Emerson (1803-1882); a famous writer and founding member of the Transcendentalists at Brook Farm. His family also owned many homes, one of which Hawthorne and his family lived in for three years.
38. Assabeth - a river in Concord, Massachusetts
39. Ellery Channing - William Ellery Channing (1818-1901); a young poet who stayed briefly at Brook Farm at the same time Hawthorne was there.
40. Thoreau - Henry David Thoreau (1817-1862); a Transcendentalist writer, famous for *Walden* (see #41)
41. Walden - (1854) a non-fiction book about Henry David Thoreau's experience while living in a self-built cabin on the shore of Walden Pond outside of Concord, Massachusetts

42. Longfellow - Henry Wadsworth Longfellow (1807-1882); Hawthorne's former classmate at Bowdoin College; famous for his great American poetry and for writing the first American translation of Dante's *Divine Comedy*

43. Hillard - George Stillman Hillard (1808-1879); a lawyer from Boston who offered political and financial aid to Hawthorne

44. Alcott - Amos Bronson Alcott (1799-1888); the father of famous writer, Louisa May Alcott; a philosopher and teacher who is best remembered for founding his own Utopian community called "Fruitlands"

45. Burns - Robert Burns (1759-1796); a poet and lyricist from Scotland who also served briefly as an excise officer in a custom house

46. Chaucer - Geoffrey Chaucer (1343-1400); a famous English writer, remembered mostly for *The Canterbury Tales*; also served as custom officer in London for many years

47. Naval Officer - an officer of the Navy who holds a position of power in which he is given direct authority by way of the governing power in place

48. Napoleon - Napoleon Bonaparte (1769-1821); a general during the French Revolution

49. Shakespeare - William Shakespeare (1564-1616); an English playwright and poet, thought of by most scholars as the greatest writer of the English language

50. Billy Gray - wealthy Salem sea merchant in the late eighteenth and nineteenth centuries

51. Simon Forrester - wealthy Salem sea merchant in the late eighteenth and nineteenth centuries

52. Halifax - the capital of the Canadian province of Nova Scotia

53. protectorate - a smaller sovereign state that agrees to enter a relationship with a stronger country or region in agreement for protection and aid

54. Governor (William) Shirley - colonial governor of Massachusetts from 1741-1749 and 1753-1756

55. Jonathan Pue - (?-1760); Hawthorne's early predecessor in the post of Salem Custom House surveyor.

56. Province of Massachusetts Bay - one of the first colonies in the New World

57. Felt's Annals - *The Annals of Salem from Its First Settlement,* written by Joseph B. Felt; annals are historical written records kept in chronological order

58. St. Peter's Church - reference to the church in the Vatican City where the Catholic Pope presides

59. Weigher - a person in a custom house who weighs packages/imports.

60. Gauger - an inspector in a custom house who checks the dimensions and quality of packages/imports

61. anthracite - a form of coal that is shiny and has the highest carbon content with the fewest impurities

62. General Taylor - Zachariah Taylor (1784-1850); a military general who was later elected President of the United States under the Whig party. Upon entering his office, he removed Hawthorne from his post at the Custom House.

63. Democrats - members of the Democratic political party

64. Irving's Headless Horseman - a reference to *The Legend of Sleepy Hollow* (1820) by Washington Irving (1783-1859). In the story, the protagonist, Ichabod Crane, is chased by the ghost of a headless horseman.

Chapter One

1. utopia - a non-existent place where the political, social, and economic systems in place are fair and just and seek to serve the best interests of the people

2. Isaac Johnson - (1803-1853); one of the first Boston settlers; upon his death he was buried on his own farm, which later became a cemetery

3. New World - the New England colonies and the rest of America that was not yet discovered

4. burdock - a vegetable plant that can be eaten or used for medicinal purposes

5. pigweed - a weedy plant that is mostly used as pig food

6. apple peru - known today as datura; a plant that can be highly poisonous and can lead to delirium if eaten

7. Ann Hutchinson - religious leader who claimed that faith, not good works, brought people closer to God; held Bible study meetings in which she proclaimed her own beliefs about Scripture and was later tried for heresy and excommunicated

Chapter Two

1. Antinomian - a religious group that believed God's laws existed in faith and not in the laws made up by the church or society

2. Quaker - a believer in the religious sect of Christianity developed in the 1700s by George Fox, who focused on the individual's relationship and growth with God

3. firewater - the Native American people's name for the "white man's" alcohol

4. Mistress Hibbins - Ann Hibbins, who was hanged in 1656 in Salem for being a witch

5. gallows - a wooden frame that is used for public hangings

6. farthingale - a slip worn under a woman's dress that gave a skirt a puffy appearance

7. "manlike" Elizabeth - reference to Queen Elizabeth I (1533-1603) and the common perception of her stern and unfeminine appearance and behavior

8. Ale - a drink similar to beer

9. far-off island - in this case, Hawthorne is referring to England

10. malefactress - one who does deliberate wrong or evil

11. magistrates - judicial officers; those who make and enforce laws
12. autumnal - past maturity; in the middle of life
13. Scripture - the Bible
14. statute-book - a book that contains the laws and regulations of a community
15. beadle - a minor church official who ushers or helps preserve order during services
16. staff of office - the symbol of a person's rank and position in the local government
17. sumptuary - a type of law that focuses on personal behavior
18. an hour past meridian - literally, an hour past the middle, or 1 o' clock
19. guillotine among the terrorists of France - reference to the French Revolution and to those who were responsible for putting many innocent people to death by way of the guillotine
20. Papist - a term, usually derogatory, that refers to followers of the Roman Catholic religion
21. Divine Maternity - a reference to the Virgin Mary, the mother of Jesus, from the Bible
22. Elizabethan ruff - a neckpiece or collar made of lace, worn in the 16th and 17th centuries

Chapter Three
1. Daniel - a Biblical Prophet who interpreted dreams and received visions
2. Governor Bellingham – Richard Bellingham (1592-1672); became governor of colonial Massachusetts in 1641, removed from office in 1642 after he married his friend's fiancée, causing a scandal
3. Divine institutions - reference to the those beliefs that are held holy
4. John Wilson - a prominent opponent of Ann Hutchinson and a preacher at First Church in Boston
5. skullcap - a small cloth headcover worn by religious leaders

Chapter Four
1. savage people - Native Americans/American Indians
2. "drive Satan out of her with stripes" - "with stripes" means to whip with leather straps or cords; in this case, they mean to draw the devil out of her soul by whipping her so hard the devil cannot even handle the beating
3. draught - a drink; often referring to beer
4. "Lethe nor Nepenthe" - Lethe is one of the rivers of Hades in Greek mythology which causes anyone who enters it to forget their former life; Nepenthe was a drug from Greek mythology which was believed to help people forget their sorrows. In the context, Chillingworth cannot erase or make Hester forget the bad things that have happened to her.
5. Paracelsus - an alchemist, physician, astrologer, and occultist during 16th Century
6. "Black Man" - the devil

Chapter Five
1. Oriental - referring to the style that comes from Asia and the Mideast; beautiful and ornate decoration and detail
2. "branded the brow of Cain" - Biblical reference to the story of Cain and Abel in which Cain kills his brother and is then cursed to wander the Earth with the mark of his sin always upon him. The mark itself has many interpretations, including the form of a scar or a curse which prevents him from cultivating crops.
3. Sabbath - the day, usually Sunday, observed for God and religious worship
4. Universal Father - God

Chapter Six
1. Eden - refers to The Garden of Eden from the Bible
2. "world's first parents" - Adam and Eve from the Bible; believed to be the first humans on earth
3. Scriptural - referring to any authority or direction that comes directly out of the Bible
4. sprite - a creature from fantasy, such as an elf or fairy
5. Quakers - believers in the religious sect of Christianity developed in the 1700s by George Fox; believe that faith and belief in God do not rely on interception by religious clergy or sacraments and instead focus on the individual's relationship and growth with God
6. sham-fight - pretend fighting/battles
7. Luther - Martin Luther (1483-1546); a German monk and church reformer considered to be the founder of Protestantism

Chapter Seven
1. Aladdin - reference to a medieval Arabian story in which a poor young man named Aladdin comes into possession of a magic lamp which houses a genie that can grant him whatever he wishes
2. Chronicles of England - *The Chronicles of England, Scotland, and Ireland* (1577) written by Raphael Holinshed (?-1580) and many other contributors; a detailed account of each of the countries' geographical and historical information
3. cuirass, gorget, greaves, gauntlets - breastplate, steel collar, leg armor, and protective gloves
4. panoply - complete suit of armor
5. Pequod (also spelled Pequot) War - an armed conflict in 1637 in which New England forces and their allies battled against the Pequot tribe, killing more than 600 from the tribe.
6. Bacon, Coke, Noye, Finch - Francis Bacon, Edward Coke, William Noye, and John Finch were all famous British lawyers during the 16th and 17th centuries

7. Mr. Blackstone - one of the first British settlers to come to the New World; legend says that he planted rose bushes and apples trees

Chapter Eight

1. King James - a reference to the style of clothing worn during the reign of King James from 1566-1625. As successor of Elizabeth I, Kind James was of the House of Stuarts, and was ruler of England, Scotland and Ireland all at once; commissioned the *King James Version* translation of the Bible
2. John the Baptist - a Jewish preacher from the 1st century who was considered to be one of the first who recognized Jesus as the Messiah. He is said to be Jesus' cousin and the person who baptized Jesus
3. English Church - The Church of England; the Puritans revolted against The Church of England before going to the New World
4. Lord of Misrule - an official job during medieval times; a person who was responsible for keeping order; a police officer of medieval times
5. bedizen - to dress or decorate ornately
6. Catechism - the beginning stages of religious instruction for the young and for those who are new to the religion; also, a summary of the doctrine taught by the Christian faith, which is meant to be memorized or at least well known
7. Babylon - a Biblical reference to the Whore of Babylon (a city in ancient Mesopotamia) who wears purple and scarlet and was decked with precious stones such as pearls
8. pearl of great price - referring to a parable told by Jesus about Heaven
9. New England Primer - a textbook that introduced the alphabet and reading to children through pictures and Biblical rhymes
10. Westminster Catechism - a book that taught basic theology to children as well as adults
11. mountebank - a person who tricks people into buying a fake product
12. Mistress Hibbins - a non-fictional woman who was hanged in Salem for being a witch

Chapter Nine

1. Atlantic - The Atlantic Ocean, the ocean that divides England from the New World
2. Elixir of Life - a legendary potion that gives the drinker eternal life
3. European pharmacopoeia - a book that explains how to mix and compose medicines
4. Oxford - a city in England, which is also home to Oxford University, the oldest university in the English-speaking world
5. Sir Kenelm Digby - (1603-1665) famous alchemist and astrologer
6. New Jerusalem - also known as a heavenly Jerusalem; according to the Christian Bible, the earthly location where true believers of Christ will spend all of eternity with God after the second creation of the world
7. Gobelin looms - tapestries created by the Gobelin family in the 16th Century which depicted Biblical scenes
8. David and Bathsheba; Nathan the Prophet - Biblical reference to King David, who has an affair with Bathsheba, a wife of one of his soldiers, Uriah. Nathan, a Prophet of God, spoke out against David's adultery
9. Sir Thomas Overbury (1581-1613) Doctor Forman- an English poet and essayist who was murdered for opposing the marriage of the earl of Rochester to the countess of Essex; (Forman was an old alchemist who provided the poison for Overbury's death)

Chapter Ten

1. Bunyan - John Bunyan (1628-1688), the author of *Pilgrim's Progress*, who referred to the side of a hill as the entrance to Hell
2. Holy Writ - Biblical Scripture

Chapter Eleven

1. Pentecost/Tongues of Flame - a Christian holiday in which God gave the apostles a tongue of flame that allowed them to speak in all different languages and still understand each other
2. Enoch - Biblical reference to a direct descendant of Adam and ancestor of Noah
3. penance - in some Christian churches, self punishment for sin; an act of atonement that is imposed on a person by a clergyman after their ritual confession of sins

Chapter Twelve

1. Geneva Cloak - a black cloak worn by Calvinist ministers
2. hieroglyphics - an ancient Egyptian writing system that uses symbols or pictures
3. sexton - a church caretaker

Chapter Thirteen

1. sick-chamber - a specific room in which the sick or elderly are roomed so that they can be better tended and not spread illness and disease

Chapter Fifteen

1. Hornbook - an early text that taught the alphabet by depicting each letter with a scene or character from the Bible

Chapter Sixteen

1. scrofula - a form of tuberculosis most common in children

Chapter Twenty

1. Old World - referring to Europe, or in this case, England
2. Spanish Main - what is today the Caribbean; in the 16th Century this included Florida, Mexico, Central American, and the northern coast of South America
3. Bristol - a city in southwest England
4. Election Sermon - the homily given on the day the new governor of the province is to be formally instated into office
5. weathercock - a weather vane; an object placed on the roof of a home that turns easily to see the direction of the wind
6. Paradise - Christian heaven
7. Ann Turner - responsible for poisoning Sir Thomas Overbury (see #9 in Chapter Nine); hanged in the style of clothes she popularized (starched collars and cuffs)
8. Apostle Eliot - John Eliot; translated the Bible into the Indian dialects so that the Indian tribes surrounding the English towns could read Scripture, and therefore, convert to Christianity
9. Hebrew - language spoken by Israelites and Jews all over the world; also the language spoken and written in the Old Testament of the Christian Bible
10. Moses - a Hebrew leader in the Bible who led the Israelites out of slavery and brought the 10 Commandments from God to the people
11. New Jerusalem - also known as a heavenly Jerusalem; according to the Christian Bible, the earthly location where true believers of Christ will spend all of eternity with God after the second creation of the world

Chapter Twenty-One

1. plebeian - common person
2. Merry Andrew - a clown or a buffoon
3. Cornwall and Devonshire - neighboring parts of England
4. aqua-vitae - a strong liquor, often used to "revive" spirits or wake a person from fainting

Chapter Twenty-Two

1. College of Arms - an establishment that records, grants, and regulates heraldry, armorial bearings, and pedigrees; started in 1484 by Kind Richard III
2. Knights Templar - famous Christian military order that was created to protect the pilgrims who traveled to Jerusalem after the First Crusade
3. Bradstreet, Endicott, Dudley, Bellingham - Simon Bradstreet, John Endicott, Thomas Dudley, Richard Bellingham were all governors of New England in the 17th Century
4. House of Peers - members of the House of Peers were representatives from Scotland and Ireland who were chosen to go to England and represent their own country in the House of Lords
5. Privy Council - cabinet members who advise the head of state or monarch
6. Indian powwow - a gathering of Native Americans/American Indians in which singing, dancing, and socializing takes place
7. Lapland wizard - a fictional wizard of tales from the Province of Lapland, Finland
8. Increase Mather – Puritan minister who assisted in the establishment of Harvard University and also took part in the Salem Witch Trials. Wrote "The Return of Several Ministers Consulted" in which he urged judges of the Salem Witch Trials to use moderation when considering unproven evidence such as dreams and visions as proof of witchcraft. However, because he never denounced the judge's actions in the Trials, his reputation became tarnished.

Chapter Twenty-Three

1. Eternal Justice - reference to Judgement Day; or the day in which the dead are sent to Heaven or to Hell for eternity

Chapter Twenty-Four

1. Infinite Purity - use of synecdoche referring to God

Name _____ Period_____

Vocabulary List

The Scarlet Letter is full of rich, complex vocabulary that you may not be particularly familiar with. Hawthorne's command of language and descriptive word choice makes _The Scarlet Letter_ a classic American novel.

Directions: Use a dictionary or the author's words to find the meanings of the following words from _The Scarlet Letter_. Your teacher will direct you to do this lesson either as you read each chapter, or as a pre-reading activity. Whatever method your teacher chooses, be sure to keep this list and your definitions to use in vocabulary exercises and to study for quizzes and tests.

Chapters 1-3
1. beadle
2. contumely
3. ignominy
4. inauspicious
5. mien
6. physiognomies
7. pillory
8. remonstrance
9. sagacity
10. vie

Chapters 4-6
1. anathemas
2. draught
3. efficacy
4. expostulation
5. gesticulation
6. paramour
7. phantasmagoric
8. quaff
9. sable
10. uncongenial

Chapters 7-9
1. cabalistic
2. chirurgical
3. contagion
4. deportment
5. despondent
6. emaciated
7. erudition
8. imperious
9. leech
10. pestilence

Chapters 10-12
1. demerits
2. ethereal
3. expiation
4. inextricable
5. inimical
6. ominous
7. portent
8. scurrilous
9. somnambulism
10. zenith

Chapters 13-15
1. asperity
2. austerity
3. despotic
4. effluence
5. enigma
6. gibe
7. innate
8. petulant
9. proffered
10. requital

Chapters 16-18
1. colloquy
2. consecration
3. denizen
4. dryad
5. harrowed
6. hillock
7. loquacity
8. meditative
9. transmuting
10. vestige

Chapters 19-21
1. depredation
2. disquietude
3. jocularity
4. languor
5. obeisance
6. potentate
7. prattle
8. preternatural
9. uncouth
10. vicissitude

Chapters 22-24
1. apotheosize
2. audacity
3. contiguous
4. erratic
5. gait
6. indefatigable
7. morion
8. necromancy
9. pathos
10. repugnance

Name _____ Period_____

Prior Knowledge Assessment Activity: Part One

Directions: *Based on your previous knowledge and what you have read in the Author Biography and the articles on Historical Context, fill in each blank with the correct answer.*

Part One

1. Nathaniel Hawthorne was famous for being part of the _____Movement.

2. Hawthorne was one of the first authors to explore the _____ and _____of his characters.

3. Most of Hawthorne's work is remembered for _____

_____ .

4. Hawthorne's ancestors were some of the first to _____ .

5. Hawthorne's great-grandfather was a _____during the _____ .

6. Two of Hawthorne's most famous friends include _____and

_____ .

7. To pay his bills, Nathaniel Hawthorne worked at the _____ .

8. Hawthorne also joined the _____Movement and lived on

_____, a utopian farming community.

9. On July 9, 1842, Hawthorne married_____, a fellow

_____ .

10. The newly married Hawthorne and his wife moved into_____, one

of the homes owned by _____.

11. Hawthorne and his wife had _____children; the eldest, _____, was the

inspiration for the character of _____from *The Scarlet Letter*.

12. _____was one author who valued Hawthorne's writing and even

dedicated his most famous novel, _____, to Hawthorne.

13. Hawthorne later bought the former home of Louisa May Alcott's family and changed its

name from _____to _____ .

14. When _____was elected President of the United States,

Hawthorne was appointed _____and was therefore forced to live

in _____ .

15. When Hawthorne finally moved back to the United States he started to write his final novel,

_____, for which he had collected materials

while traveling.

Name _____ Period _____

Prior Knowledge Assessment Activity: Part Two

Directions: *Based on your previous knowledge and what you have read in the Author Biography and the articles on Historical Context, fill in each blank with the correct answer.*

Part Two

1. A Puritan is _____.

2. When the Puritans fought for religious reform, they were opposed by the _____ , King _____ , and King _____.

3. The Puritans wanted church services to focus on _____, _____ , and _____.

4. Out of the conflict between the Church of England and the Puritans, a new translation of the Bible was developed, which is known as the _____.

5. The revolution against the Church of England was led by _____.

6. The Puritans who did not want to revolt against the church came to the New World and signed the _____.

7. _____ and _____ were intertwined in Puritan society because the _____ norms and_____ codes were parallel.

8. Puritan life was centered on _____ and _____.

9. Everyone in Puritan society worked hard because their lives were _____ and they worked _____ so that they could prosper as a _____ .

10. Any form of _____ from social norms was seen as dissention from the laws set forth by _____, and was therefore punishable.

11. Punishment was mainly centered on _____, and the idea of _____.

12. A popular punishment was to be placed on the _____ while being trapped in a wooden _____.

13. The only way to get out of punishment was to declare the _____, which required the accused read a passage from the _____ without mistakes.

14. Because their survival rested heavily on the graciousness of God, the underlying fear that gripped the Puritans was _____.

15. When something or someone acted strange or could not be explained, it was simply blamed on _____, and many were accused of _____, which later led to mass hysteria and _____.

16. The majority of society was made up of _____.

17. Only men were allowed to take _____ roles in society; women were considered a man's _____.

Active Reading Guide: Note-Taking and Summarizing

Nathaniel Hawthorne was well-known for his skillful development of his characters and their psychology. To understand and appreciate Hawthorne's characterization, you will be keeping notes on the actions and motivations of the three main characters in *The Scarlet Letter*. As you read each section, complete the Active Reading Guide, taking notes using short phrases and bullet points.

☑ **Plot Points**: for each character, note major actions and how the actions contribute to the overall plot
☑ **Motivation**: for each character, whether is it clearly stated in the novel or not, indicate why you think the character does what he/she does (or says).
☑ **Prediction**: based on the actions and motivation of each character, write what you think they will do in the next section of the novel
☑ **Connection**: for each character, write how you identify, or do not identify, with their actions, behavior, and motivation. How does the situation that the character is in make you feel? Do you empathize with the character or not?
☑ **Questions**: write down any questions you have about any of the characters or about anything you read and did not understand

	Prynne	**Dimmesdale**	**Chillingworth**
Plot Points	*In this space, write what each character does in the section that is worthy of note. Where do they go? Who do they meet? What decisions are made?* Ex. *Chapter 7:* • Hester goes to Governor Bellingham's house to return a pair of gloves • she notices her reflection in a suit of armor which makes the scarlet letter seem magnified and overwhelming • Hester tries to calm Pearl when she wants a rose from the garden		
Motivation	*In this space, write why they acted the way they did. What spurs them to move forward? Why do they do the things they do?* Ex. *Chapter 7:* • Hester wants to talk to Bellingham about rumors she has heard about Pearl being taken away from her.		
Prediction	*In this space, write what you think will happen next based on the things that happened in this section, giving the reasons behind your prediction.* Ex. *Chapter 7:* • Hester will get to keep Pearl and have to teach her about the Puritan way of life.		
Connection	*In this space, write how you feel about each character and their actions. Do you think they are right or wrong? Do you empathize with them?* Ex. *Chapter 7:* • I feel bad for Hester. I don't think they should take Pearl away from her because she is her real mother and she has a right to raise her any way she wants.		
Questions	*In this space, include any questions you have about anything you read in this section and about any of the characters. Also, feel free to use this space to make note of any comments that you find interesting or important as you read.* Ex. *Chapter 7:* • page. 94: "It was the scarlet letter in another form; the scarlet letter endowed with life!" (author talking about Pearl)		

Name _____ Period_____

Comprehension Check: The Custom House

Directions: *After reading "The Custom House Introductory" and the short summary below, answer the following questions in complete sentences on a separate sheet of paper.*

In the introduction of *The Scarlet Letter*, Hawthorne gives a semi-autobiographical account of his time working at the Salem Custom House. He also explains the history of his prominent ancestors and states that they would have been ashamed of his decision to be a writer, because it was not viewed as a career deserving of social respect. As he talks about the men that he worked with, Hawthorne goes into great detail explaining how they looked, how they spoke, and about their personalities and backgrounds. This aspect of the introduction exemplifies Hawthorne's talent for characterization and in-depth character description. Another important part of the introduction talks about Hawthorne finding abandoned papers and a rag cut into the shape of an A. The papers told the story of a woman named Hester Prynne and her connection to the rag. Hawthorne then explains to the reader that he has tried to recreate her story as factually as possible. Finally, Hawthorne explains how he was kicked out of his position as Surveyor at the Custom House when President Taylor came into office, which then allowed him to focus his attention on Hester Prynne's story.

1. Why is it important to read the introduction before reading the rest of the novel?

2. What is significant about Hawthorne's mention of his ancestors in the introduction to the novel?

3. What does the focus on the Custom House and the description of his fellow workers reveal about Hawthorne?

4. Why do you think Hawthorne decided to write his introduction rather than including this information in the plotline of the story?

5. What is the importance of Hawthorne telling the audience about finding the papers and the tattered rag referring to Hester Prynne?

6. From the information given in the *Introductory* alone, write a 3-5 sentence prediction of what you think the story will be about.

7. How does Hawthorne feel about the new political party taking over at the end of the introduction? What are his political beliefs and affiliations?

Name _____ Period_____

Chapters 1 – 3
Active Reading Guide

Directions: As you read Chapters 1-3 of **The Scarlet Letter**, examine each character's motivation and actions, completing the chart below. For help, refer to page 25.

	Prynne	Dimmesdale	Chillingworth
Plot Points			
Motivation			
Prediction			
Connection			
Questions			

Chapters 1 – 3
Comprehension Check

Directions: *As you read each chapter, answer the following questions on a separate piece of paper using complete sentences.*

Chapter 1

1. What does Hawthorne describe in detail in this first chapter? Write a short description of it in your own words.

2. What were the first two things the Puritans built upon arriving to the new colony? What does this reveal about the needs and views of Puritan culture?

3. What does the narrator say he hopes the rose bush will symbolize? In your own words, what can you predict about the ending of the novel based upon this statement?

Chapter 2

1. Why are all the townspeople gathered in the center of town?

2. Describe how the women in New England are different from the generations of women before them.

3. What is Hester Prynne's relationship to Arthur Dimmesdale?

4. Describe Hester Prynne.

5. What is Hester's crime? What does the letter *A* stand for?

6. Why were the women upset when they saw Hester's embroidered letter?

7. What is the scaffold? What is it used for?

8. What is on Hester's mind as she serves out the first part of her punishment?

Chapter 3

1. What does Hester notice immediately about the strange man being accompanied by an Indian?

2. What gesture does the stranger make to Hester when he realizes that she recognizes him?

3. What does the stranger tell one of the townspeople about himself?

4. What does the townsman tell the stranger about Hester's crime? What do we learn about Hester's husband?

5. Describe Reverend Dimmesdale.

6. What do the magistrates and ministers want Hester to tell them? What does she do?

7. What does Dimmesdale do and say after Hester firmly states that she will not reveal the name of her lover?

Chapters 1 – 3
Standards Focus: Allusions

An **allusion** is an implied or indirect reference to a person, event, or another text. Allusions are included in literature with the assumption that the reader and the author share a common knowledge, and therefore the reader will understand the reference. Most allusions in Western literature come from the Bible, mythology, or other Western literature.

Allusions conjure images of various characters or events that are linked to a specific idea and can be used to tie together a past issue with a current one. An allusion can be anything from the mention of a name to a line of a song, as an author uses the reference to make his point clearer. However, if the reader does not know the allusion to which the author is referring, the effect of the allusion is lost and the point of the reference may be missed.

Allusions are used not only in literature, but also in films, speeches, poetry, and even common, everyday dialogue. For example, maybe you know a person who is stingy and grumpy when Christmas time rolls around. You might say something to them like, "Oh, John, don't be such a Scrooge." Maybe you have said this before and not even realized you were giving an allusion to a character from Charles Dickens's novel, *A Christmas Carol*.

Directions: *Answer the questions below on a separate sheet of paper using complete sentences.*

1. Read the list of allusions from *The Scarlet Letter (pages 17-21)*. Have you heard of any of these allusions? Are there some references with which you are more familiar than others? Take a look specifically at the allusions found in Chapters 1-3. Choose three allusions, and then explain the reference and how it is appropriate at that point in the novel. Why do you think Hawthorne included each of these in his novel?

2. What is important about the allusion Hawthorne makes about Mistress Hibbins?

3. Have you heard any of the allusions made in or about *The Scarlet Letter* in any other contexts, such as in another book, speech, or part of history? Where and in what context? Make a prediction about how these allusions may affect The Scarlet Letter.

4. Name some other allusions that you have heard or read about in literature. What was their context and significance? Why was an allusion appropriate at that particular moment? If necessary, thumb through a novel or two you have already read.

5. Why are allusions sometimes more effective than simply explaining a situation more thoroughly? What are the pros and cons of using allusions?

Chapters 1 – 3
Assessment Preparation: Definitions

Directions: *Complete the assignment by using a dictionary to (a.) find the vocabulary word's part of speech, (b.) define the word, and (c.) use the word in an original sentence.*

1. inauspicious

    a. part of speech: _____

    b. definition: _____

    _____

    c. sentence: _____

    _____

2. physiognomy

    a. part of speech: _____

    b. definition: _____

    _____

    c. sentence: _____

    _____

3. beadle

    a. part of speech: _____

    b. definition: _____

    _____

    c. sentence: _____

    _____

4. pillory

    a. part of speech: _____

    b. definition: _____

    _____

    c. sentence: _____

    _____

5. ignominy

    a. part of speech: _____

    b. definition: _____

    _____

    c. sentence: _____

_____

6. mien

    a. part of speech: _____

    b. definition: _____

_____

    c. sentence: _____

_____

7. vie

    a. part of speech: _____

    b. definition: _____

_____

    c. sentence: _____

_____

8. remonstrance

    a. part of speech: _____

    b. definition: _____

_____

    c. sentence: _____

_____

9. contumely

    a. part of speech: _____

    b. definition: _____

_____

    c. sentence: _____

_____

10. sagacity

    a. part of speech: _____

    b. definition: _____

_____

    c. sentence: _____

_____

Chapters 4 – 6
Active Reading Guide

Directions: *As you read Chapters 4-6 of* **The Scarlet Letter***, examine each character's motivation and actions, completing the chart below. For help, refer to page 25.*

	Prynne	Dimmesdale	Chillingworth
Plot Points			
Motivation			
Prediction			
Connection			
Questions			

Chapters 4 – 6
Comprehension Check

Directions: *As you read each chapter, answer the following questions on a separate piece of paper using complete sentences.*

Chapter 4

1. Why was Hester placed under constant watch when she returned to the prison?
2. What is the stranger's name and what is his relationship to Hester?
3. Chillingworth says that he and Hester have both wronged each other. What is his reasoning behind this?
4. What does he ask Hester to promise him? Why do you think he asks this of her?
5. What does he promise to do if Hester does not freely reveal the name of her lover?
6. What is Chillingworth's response when Hester asks him why he won't just announce himself and cast her off?

Chapter 5

1. Why does Hester decide to stay close to her town instead of going back to Europe or joining another community?
2. How does Hester make money? (What is her gift?)
3. What is ironic about the townspeople's willingness to purchase Hester's creations?
4. How does Hester dress and act?
5. How is she treated by the townspeople? Who does she dread the most? Why?
6. What happens when Hester looks into the eyes of the townspeople who stare at the scarlet letter on her bosom?

Chapter 6

1. Why did Hester name her child "Pearl"?
2. Describe how Pearl is dressed. What reason is given for the way Pearl is dressed?
3. What thoughts does Hester have about Pearl? How does Pearl react to punishment?
4. What is Pearl's relationship with the other children of the town? Why do you believe this is so?
5. Who are Pearl's playmates? What does she do to entertain herself?
6. Do you think Hester is a martyr, or do you think her repentance is sincere? Explain.

Chapters 4 – 6
Standards Focus: Characterization

One of the important elements of fiction is **characterization**: the process by which a character is given human characteristics and personality. Basically, the author creates a character that possesses as many human qualities as possible, making the character seem like a real and tangible person. Hawthorne took an especially interesting twist by including the psychology of the characters as part of their characterization. Although many authors had used the thoughts of characters as part of their characterization technique, no one had delved into the emotions and motivations as deeply as Hawthorne did in *The Scarlet Letter*. By allowing the reader to "see" into the inner thoughts and emotions working in the minds of his characters, audiences are not just told about the actions of the character, but also learn about their inner motivations and why the character behaves in a certain way.

There are many aspects that go into good characterization and many classifications of a character. First, there is the way the audience learns about a character: directly or indirectly. **Direct** characterization is when the author tells the audience what the character is like, through a narrator, another character, or even through the speech of the character himself. **Indirect** characterization is made when the reader has to decide for themselves what the character is like; for example, by dialogue, actions, thoughts, or interaction with other characters.

Another aspect of characterization is the development of character type. There are two major classifications of character types: **flat** versus **round** and **dynamic** versus **static**. A **flat** character is one in which only a few human attributes are given, making them more of a background character or a symbolic character who does not have major involvement in the central plot. A flat character usually has one major trait which he/she carries throughout the novel and on which the author focuses. However, a **round** character is one that has many human qualities and that shows a range of emotions, actions, and motivations. Round characters are usually the main focus of the novel because they show growth and change over the course of the novel and because readers can more easily relate to their humanness.

The other type of classification, dynamic versus static, comes from studying a character arc. A **character arc** is a literary device that allows the reader to keep track of the change a character goes through in the story. A **static** character is the same at the beginning of the novel as he/she was at the beginning, not having learned from the experiences undergone during the novel. A **dynamic** character, on the other hand, is one that changes opinions or ideas and grows from the beginning to the end of the novel. The **protagonist**, the main character, is almost always a dynamic character because he or she undergoes the most change of anyone in the novel. The **antagonist** is the character that stands in the way of the protagonist's goal. Although it is easy to qualify the antagonist as "the bad guy," this is not always the case. Often, the antagonist and protagonist are hard to tell apart because both can be likeable characters.

One more important element of characterization is the **naming** of characters. As is clear in *The Scarlet Letter*, many names can evoke a certain thought or feeling. For example, the name Chillingworth brings to mind a coldness and harshness that is synonymous with his character. It is no accident that a character's name is reflective of his or her personality. Often, an author will deliberately choose a name that sounds like what he or she wants the character to be, because a character's name says a lot about him and is one of the main influences on the reader's thoughts about the character. A character's name can tell the reader where the character is from and his social status, and can even set the tone for how the audience should feel about him or her.

Name _____ Period_____

Chapters 4 – 6
Standards Focus: Characterization Activity

Directions: Complete the chart below by filling in the characterization qualification for each box. For the last two columns, complete with examples from the text as indicated.

	Static or Dynamic?	Round or Flat?	Protagonist or Antagonist?	Give one example of how each character is *directly* characterized (include page number and description)	Give one example of how each character is *indirectly* characterized (include page number and description)
Hester Prynne					
Pearl					
Arthur Dimmesdale					
Roger Chillingworth					
Mistress Hibbons					
The Townspeople					

Chapters 4 – 6
Assessment Preparation: Word Origins

Directions: *Using your vocabulary list and a dictionary, find (a) the vocabulary word with the same root as the example, (b) two other words that share the same root, and (c) the definition of the vocabulary word.*

1. The word <u>draft</u> comes from the Old English *drōht*, meaning "to pull."

    a. Which vocabulary word has the same root? _____

    b. List two other words that have the same root:

    _____   _____

    c. Definition of the vocabulary word: _____

    _____

2. The word <u>efficient</u> comes from the Latin *efficiantia*, meaning "enough of."

    a. Which vocabulary word has the same root? _____

    b. List two other words that have the same root:

    _____   _____

    c. Definition of the vocabulary word: _____

    _____

3. The word <u>qualify</u> comes from the Latin *qual*, meaning "of what sort."

    a. Which vocabulary word has the same root? _____

    b. List two other words that have the same root:

    _____   _____

    c. Definition of the vocabulary word: _____

    _____

4. The word <u>exposure</u> comes from the Latin *expostulare*, meaning "demand urgently."

    a. Which vocabulary word has the same root? _____

    b. List two other words that have the same root:

    _____   _____

    c. Definition of the vocabulary word: _____

    _____

5. The word <u>paramount</u> comes from the Middle English *par amour*, meaning "with love."

    a. Which vocabulary word has the same root? _____

    b. List two other words that have the same root:

    _____   _____

c. Definition of the vocabulary word: _____

_____

6. The word <u>congeal</u> comes from the Latin *con genius*, meaning "compatible."

   a. Which vocabulary word has the same root? _____

   b. List two other words that have the same root:

_____   _____

   c. Definition of the vocabulary word: _____

_____

7. The word <u>sabotage</u> comes from the Slavic *sobol*, meaning "black."

   a. Which vocabulary word has the same root? _____

   b. List two other words that have the same root:

_____   _____

   c. Definition of the vocabulary word: _____

_____

8. The word <u>anathematic</u> comes from the Greek *anathé*, meaning "a thing accursed."

   a. Which vocabulary word has the same root? _____

   b. List two other words that have the same root:

_____   _____

   c. Definition of the vocabulary word: _____

_____

9. The word <u>phantastron</u> comes from the Greek *phantasm*, meaning an "image or vision."

   a. Which vocabulary word has the same root? _____

   b. List two other words that have the same root:

_____   _____

   c. Definition of the vocabulary word: _____

_____

10. The word <u>gestic</u> comes from the Latin *gestus*, meaning "having made mimic gestures."

   a. Which vocabulary word has the same root? _____

   b. List two other words that have the same root:

_____   _____

   c. Definition of the vocabulary word: _____

_____

Chapters 7 – 9
Active Reading Guide

Directions: As you read Chapters 7-9 of **The Scarlet Letter**, examine each character's motivation and actions, completing the chart below. For help, refer to page 25.

	Prynne	Dimmesdale	Chillingworth
Plot Points			
Motivation			
Prediction			
Connection			
Questions			

Chapters 7 – 9
Comprehension Check

Directions: As you read each chapter, answer the following questions on a separate piece of paper using complete sentences.

Chapter 7

1. Why does Hester go to the Governor's house?
2. What does the author say is remarkable about Pearl and her clothes?
3. Who do Hester and Pearl encounter on their way to the Governor's house? What interaction takes place?
4. Briefly describe the Governor's hall.
5. What does Pearl want from the Governor's garden? What does she do when she doesn't get it? What stops her behavior?

Chapter 8

1. Who is with the Governor when he meets with Hester?
2. What does Mr. Wilson ask Pearl and what does she say?
3. Who speaks on behalf of Hester at the Governor's house? What does he say?
4. What does the Governor decide about letting Hester raise Pearl? Explain.
5. Who approaches Hester when she leaves the Governor's house and what does she say?

Chapter 9

1. What is Chillingworth's position in the community?
2. How has Dimmesdale's physical appearance changed?
3. To what does Chillingworth devote all his efforts?
4. What does the window at the home that Chillingworth and Dimmesdale share look out over?
5. What physical changes is Chillingworth going through?
6. What do the townspeople think is happening to Dimmesdale?

Chapters 7 – 9
Standards Focus: Conflict

In fiction, dramatic action depends on what is known as **conflict**. Conflict, or the obstacles a character faces, is one of the most important elements of literature because conflict is what makes a character take action in the story. Since a character is facing a force of opposition, the conflict in a story makes the reader pick a side, whether it is with the protagonist or the antagonist. Without conflict, the plot of a story would simply be a sequence of events with no consequences and no interesting or exciting changes. There are three main types of conflict, at least one of which can be easily found in every novel.

- **man vs. man** – a character in the novel struggles against another character, society, or an organization
- **man vs. nature** – a character in the novel struggles against the forces of nature or fate; nature can be anything ranging from fire, to rain, to treacherous mountains, or a force as abstract as destiny
- **man vs. self** – one of the characters in the novel struggles with an internal problem that only he or she can resolve by looking inward, usually at a decision that needs to be made or at feelings that need to be worked out

Conflict is further divided into two categories: internal and external conflict. **Internal conflict** is the struggle of a character's emotions or decisions—man vs. self. **External conflict**, on the other hand, is beyond a character's control and happens externally; this includes man vs. nature and man vs. man. A conflict can also be either part of the main plot (*main conflict*), or just another obstacle on the way to the major point of the story (*subordinate conflict*).

Directions: *Complete the following exercise with evidence from the novel or from your pre-reading activities (Puritanism, Crime and Punishment in Puritan Society, or Life as a Puritan). For part a, indicate the type of conflict, and whether this conflict is internal or external. For part b, specify the opposing forces involved. For part c, choose a specific example (including source and page number) from the text(s) which clearly reveals the conflict between these opposing forces. Finally, for part d, indicate whether this conflict is a main conflict or a subordinate conflict within the plot. An example has been done for you.*

Ex. Hester stands on the scaffold as the townspeople stare and yell at her.
- a. Type of conflict/Internal or External: *man vs. man, external*
- b. Opposing Forces: *Hester versus the people of Salem*
- c. Example: *"At the very least, they should have put the brand of a hot iron on Hester Prynne's forehead." (The Scarlet Letter, pg. 47)*
- d. Main or Subordinate: *Main*

1. The Puritans try to convince the Church of England to reform.
   a. Type of Conflict/Internal or External: _____

   _____

   b. Opposing Forces: _____

   c. Example: _____

   _____

   d. Main or Subordinate: _____

Name _____ Period_____

2. The Puritans must set up a new home in a foreign land after crossing the ocean.

    a. Type of Conflict/Internal or External: _____

    _____

    b. Opposing Forces: _____

    c. Example: _____

    _____

    d. Main or Subordinate: _____

3. As Hester's punishment, she must wear the scarlet letter on her chest so she will always remember her sin and the consequences of her actions.

    a. Type of Conflict/Internal or External: _____

    _____

    b. Opposing Forces: _____

    c. Example: _____

    _____

    d. Main or Subordinate: _____

4. The Puritans think that the Indians inhabiting the areas around their town are savages.

    a. Type of Conflict/Internal or External: _____

    _____

    b. Opposing Forces: _____

    c. Example: _____

    _____

    d. Main or Subordinate: _____

5. Hester must hide Chillingworth's true identity so that she can live freely with Pearl.

    a. Type of Conflict/Internal or External: _____

    _____

    b. Opposing Forces: _____

    c. Example: _____

    _____

    d. Main or Subordinate: _____

6. Hester pleads to Governor Bellingham to allow her to keep and raise Pearl.

    a. Type of Conflict/Internal or External: _____

    _____

b. Opposing Forces: _____

c. Example: _____

_____

d. Main or Subordinate: _____

7. Dimmesdale suffers in great agony over the physical pain in his heart.

a. Type of Conflict/Internal or External: _____

_____

b. Opposing Forces: _____

c. Example: _____

_____

d. Main or Subordinate: _____

8. Hester refuses to reveal the name of her former lover to the magistrates.

a. Type of Conflict/Internal or External: _____

_____

b. Opposing Forces: _____

c. Example: _____

_____

d. Main or Subordinate: _____

9. Mistress Hibbins is convicted of being a witch and is put to death after the novel ends.

a. Type of Conflict/Internal or External: _____

_____

b. Opposing Forces: _____

c. Example: _____

_____

d. Main or Subordinate: _____

10. Chillingworth resolves to make Dimmesdale feel as guilty as possible for his sin.

a. Type of Conflict/Internal or External: _____

_____

b. Opposing Forces: _____

c. Example: _____

_____

d. Main or Subordinate: _____

Chapters 7 – 9
Assessment Preparation: Word Parts

An effective approach to figuring out the meaning of unfamiliar words is to break down the words into smaller parts. To do this, you should be familiar with common prefixes, suffixes, and base and root words. In addition, you can learn about word parts by using a dictionary. To find the correct word to look up in the dictionary, you need to pay attention to the way the word is used in the sentence. For the sample below, *relentlessly*, you would look up the base word, *relent*, since *–less* and *–ly* are both suffixes. In your dictionary, you might find more than one entry. Choose the one that most closely matches the way the word is used in context.

> ¹relent \ri-'lent\ *vb* [ME *relenten*] *vi* (1526) 1 : to become less severe, harsh, or strict usu. from reasons of humanity 2 : LET UP, SLACKEN ~ *vt, obs*: SOFTEN, MOLLIFY **syn** see yield

Look at the sample dictionary entry above. The information in the brackets [ ] is the "etymology" of the word. "ME" means that the word comes from Middle English; *relenten* is the way the word was used in Middle English. The entry (1526) tells you that the word has been in existence since 1526.

Directions: *Using a dictionary, complete the chart for Chapters 7-9 below and on the next page.*

Word	imperious	pestilence	cabalistic	contagion	chirurgical
Base	imperial				
Meaning of Base	of or relating to an empire or ruler; tyrranical				
Root and Meaning of Root	Latin: *imperium*; supreme authority; power				
Suffix(es)	-ious				
How the Suffix Changes the Word	no change: remains an adjective				

Name _____ Period _____

Word	imperious	pestilence	cabalistic	contagion	chirurgical
Inferred Meaning of Vocabulary Word	having complete power; in charge				
Vocabulary Word's Part of Speech and Dictionary Definition	Adj: arrogant; domineering; dictatorial				
Word	emaciate	despondent	deportment	leech	erudition
Base					
Meaning of Base					
Root and Meaning of Root					
Suffix(es)					
How the Suffix Changes the Word					
Inferred Meaning of Vocabulary Word					
Vocabulary Word's Part of Speech and Dictionary Definition					

Chapters 10 – 12
Active Reading Guide

Directions: As you read Chapters 10-12 of **The Scarlet Letter**, examine each character's motivation and actions, completing the chart below. For help, refer to page 25.

	Prynne	Dimmesdale	Chillingworth
Plot Points			
Motivation			
Prediction			
Connection			
Questions			

Name _____ Period _____

Chapters 10 – 12
Comprehension Check

Directions: *As you read each chapter, answer the following questions on a separate piece of paper using complete sentences.*

Chapter 10

1. What is the topic of the conversation between Dimmesdale and Chillingworth that starts a fight between them?

2. What is Dimmesdale's position on the topic?

3. What does Pearl insinuate about Chillingworth when she playfully tells Hester that they should run away from the graveyard?

4. At the end of the chapter, what does Chillingworth do to Dimmesdale and what is his reaction to what he sees?

5. What do you think he sees?

Chapter 11

1. What is Chillingworth's new obsession and devotion?

2. What do the townspeople think of Dimmesdale?

3. What does Dimmesdale resolve to do, but never acts upon?

4. Aside from Chillingworth's deliberate torment, what causes Dimmesdale to be in constant agony?

5. What does Dimmesdale do at night when he is alone?

Chapter 12

1. Where does Dimmesdale go at the beginning of the chapter? What does he do there?

2. Why are the Rev. Wilson, Hester and Pearl, and Chillingworth out in the middle of the night?

3. What happens that makes it seem like mid-day in the middle of the night?

4. Why won't Pearl tell Dimmesdale who Chillingworth is?

5. What do the townspeople think the letter *A* in the previous night's sky meant?

Chapters 10 – 12
Standards Focus: Motif

A **motif** is a symbol that appears time and again over the course of the story, reinforcing the themes of a novel. A motif can be an action, symbol, place, statement, or even an object. Although a theme and a motif sound like the same thing, the main difference is that a motif is something that supports the theme (the author's message within the novel). For example, if the theme of a novel is "the truth will eventually reveal itself," a motif from that novel might be two or three scenes that are set at night, behind which some sort of truth or secret is hidden, but is eventually revealed as day or light is seen.

Directions: To help you learn how to find and understand motifs, fill in the chart as shown in the example. First, using Chapters 1-12 of the novel, fill in the examples of the motif from the text. Then, decide what theme the motifs and examples reveal. If you need more room, continue your answers on a separate sheet of paper.

Motif	Examples of the Motif	What the Motif Reveals
Powerful or symbolic character names	Pearl was given her name because she was the "pearl of great price." Ironically, Pearl does not have the shine and luster of a pearl, but to Hester, she is very valuable and precious. Dimmesdale's name also carries great symbolism, as it is mentioned several times throughout Chapters 1-12. As his name would imply, his spirit and health are "dimming" as his sins continue to plague him. Chillingworth's name is also powerful, since his character is "chillingly" cold, heartless and deceitful as he seeks his revenge.	Character names can be important in a novel. Hawthorne was very deliberate in the names he chose for his characters. Often, authors take special care to name their characters so that their names fit and reveal their character.
The Devil / Evil		
Clothing		
Dimmesdale's hand over his heart		
Darkness and Daylight		

Chapters 10 – 12
Assessment Preparation: Connotation and Denotation

The **denotation** of a word is simply its dictionary definition. The **connotation** of a word, on the other hand, is the tone or "sound" of the word. The connotation of a word is better described as the feeling that a word provokes when read in context. Even if two words have the same definition, they may not have the same connotation. For example, a cup and a chalice are essentially the same thing, but the word chalice has a more regal and rich tone to it. A chalice is not just a cup, but an ornately decorated, jewel-covered cup, fit for a king.

Directions: *On the first line, write the definition (denotation) of the vocabulary word. On the second line, write three synonyms for the vocabulary word. Then, write a sentence using the vocabulary word and replace the word with its synonyms using the same sentence. On the last line, write which of the four words has the most negative connotation to you and why you feel this way. An example has been done for you.*

Example: ominous

Denotation: <u>having the significance of an omen of evil or harm</u>

Synonyms: <u>foreboding, threatening, portentous</u>

Sentence: <u>The darkening sky was an **ominous** sign of the coming storm.</u>
                 <u>The darkening sky was a foreboding sign of the coming storm.</u>
                 <u>The darkening sky was a threatening sign of the coming storm.</u>
                 <u>The darkening sky was a portentous sign of the coming storm.</u>

Most Negative Connotation: <u>Threatening; it gives the feeling that the danger is near.</u>

1. inimical

Denotation: _____

_____

Synonyms: _____

Sentences: _____

_____

_____

_____

Most Negative Connotation: _____

_____

2. demerits

Denotation: _____

_____

Synonyms: _____

Sentences: _____

_____

_____

_____

Name _____ Period_____

Most Negative Connotation: _____
_____

3. ethereal

Denotation: _____
_____

Synonyms: _____

Sentences: _____
_____
_____
_____

Most Negative Connotation: _____
_____

4. inextricable

Denotation: _____
_____

Synonyms: _____

Sentences: _____
_____
_____
_____

Most Negative Connotation: _____
_____

5. expiation

Denotation: _____
_____

Synonyms: _____

Sentences: _____
_____
_____
_____

Most Negative Connotation: _____
_____

6. zenith

Denotation: _____
_____

Synonyms: _____

Sentences: _____

_____

_____

_____

Most Negative Connotation: _____

_____

7. scurrilous

Denotation: _____

_____

Synonyms: _____

Sentences: _____

_____

_____

_____

Most Negative Connotation: _____

_____

8. portent

Denotation: _____

_____

Synonyms: _____

Sentences: _____

_____

_____

_____

Most Negative Connotation: _____

_____

Chapters 13 – 15
Active Reading Guide

Directions: As you read Chapters 13-15 of **The Scarlet Letter**, examine each character's motivation and actions, completing the chart below. For help, refer to page 25.

	Prynne	**Dimmesdale**	**Chillingworth**
Plot Points			
Motivation			
Prediction			
Connection			
Questions			

Chapters 13 – 15
Comprehension Check

Directions: *As you read each chapter, answer the following questions on a separate piece of paper using complete sentences.*

Chapter 13

1. After Hester's encounter with Dimmesdale on the scaffold, what worries her and what does she resolve to do about it?
2. What do the townspeople believe that the *A* on Hester's chest has begun to stand for? Why?
3. How has the attitude of the townspeople changed toward Hester?
4. What physical and psychological changes has Hester undergone?
5. How did Pearl's birth save Hester?

Chapter 14

1. When Hester and Chillingworth first meet, what does he tell her he hears is being discussed among the members of the council?
2. How does Hester respond to this?
3. What physical changes does Hester notice as she looks at Chillingworth?
4. What does Hester tell Chillingworth she wants to do?
5. What is Chillingworth's response?
6. What do you think he means by, "Let the black flower blossom as it may!"

Chapter 15

1. What does Pearl do while Hester and Chillingworth speak?
2. What does Pearl say about why Hester wears the *A*? What is the connection that she makes?
3. What is Hester's dilemma about telling Pearl the true meaning behind the scarlet letter that she wears?
4. Why does Hester say she wears the *A*? What is significant about this?
5. What does Hester do when Pearl continues to pester her about the letter?

Chapters 13 – 15
Standards Focus: Setting

The **setting** of a story is the location and time frame in which the action takes place. Setting is an important part of literature because it provides a backdrop for the story, and can often determine the actions and behaviors of the characters in the text. By knowing the setting, the audience can deduce a lot of information about the characters and story. Although there is usually one major setting for a story, for example, The Victorian Era or the Beasley family home, there are also scene settings which give the audience other specifics such as the living room, the kitchen, or the garden. There are usually many settings in a story because this helps keep the story feeling realistic and interesting.

A setting can also become a symbol of something or someone in a story, and can have a major influence on the mood and tone of a scene. The description of a setting can bring to life a vivid image of where the characters are and what is around them. For example, a scene that takes place in a dark, cold, and scary forest is very different from one that takes place in a sunny, bright, and cheerful orchard. As you can see, each of these descriptions is more useful than simply saying the scene takes place outside, among a group of trees. This kind of detailed information can help the audience understand how the character may be feeling or thinking.

Directions: *In **The Scarlet Letter**, the setting of the action is very important in evoking certain moods. Fill in the chart below by reading through the text to find scenes that take place in the specific setting indicated. Once you have found several scenes that take place in these settings, indicate how the setting is important to the scene. Also indicate what the setting may symbolize and how it is intended to make the reader feel. An example has been done for you.*

Scene	How does the setting affect the situation(s)? What is the setting a symbol of? What is the mood of the situation(s) set in these locations?
The Prison	
Ex. Hester is released from prison, forced to show her scarlet letter, and suffer humiliation from the public. (Ch. 1)	Ex. The prison may symbolize resurrection, or a new beginning, for Hester. When she leaves she is starting a new life. It is an exciting scene because there are a lot of people gathered around her, yelling at and humiliating her. I think starting the story in front of a prison is interesting and gets the audience's attention and makes the scene more exciting. It really makes the reader wonder what Hester did to deserve this punishment, and also makes the reader feel bad for her as she enters this new life as an outcast.

Scene	How does the setting affect the situation(s)? What is the setting a symbol of? What is the mood of the situation(s) set in these locations?
The Scaffold/Market Place	
The Forest	
The Governor's Hall	
Dimmesdale's & Chillingworth's House	

Chapters 13 – 15
Assessment Preparation: Definitions

Directions: *Complete the assignment by using a dictionary to (a.) the vocabulary word's part of speech (b.) its definition, and (c.) use the word in an original sentence.*

1. **gibe**

    a. part of speech: _____

    b. definition: _____

    _____

    c. sentence: _____

    _____

2. **despotic**

    a. part of speech: _____

    b. definition: _____

    _____

    c. sentence: _____

    _____

3. **austerity**

    a. part of speech: _____

    b. definition: _____

    _____

    c. sentence: _____

    _____

4. **effluence**

    a. part of speech: _____

    b. definition: _____

    _____

    c. sentence: _____

    _____

5. **proffer**

    a. part of speech: _____

    b. definition: _____

    _____

   c. sentence: _____

_____

6. petulant

   a. part of speech: _____

   b. definition: _____

_____

   c. sentence: _____

_____

7. requital

   a. part of speech: _____

   b. definition: _____

_____

   c. sentence: _____

_____

8. innate

   a. part of speech: _____

   b. definition: _____

_____

   c. sentence: _____

_____

9. enigma

   a. part of speech: _____

   b. definition: _____

_____

   c. sentence: _____

_____

10. asperity

   a. part of speech: _____

   b. definition: _____

_____

   c. sentence: _____

_____

Chapters 16 – 18
Active Reading Guide

Directions: As you read Chapters 16-18 of **The Scarlet Letter**, examine each character's motivation and actions, completing the chart below. For help, refer to page 25.

	Prynne	Dimmesdale	Chillingworth
Plot Points			
Motivation			
Prediction			
Connection			
Questions			

Chapters 16 – 18
Comprehension Check

Directions: *As you read each chapter, answer the following questions on a separate piece of paper using complete sentences.*

Chapter 16

1. What does Pearl say is the reason that the sun shines on her, but not her mother?
2. What does Pearl believe about the scarlet letter?
3. What does Pearl ask Hester when they sit and take a break in the forest?
4. What response does Hester give?
5. What comment does Pearl make about the Black Man and Dimmesdale?

Chapter 17

1. Briefly summarize what Dimmesdale tells Hester when she asks, "Is there no reality in the penitence thus sealed and witnessed by good works? And wherefore should it not bring you peace?"
2. What does Hester reveal to Dimmesdale? What is his reaction?
3. What is the threat that looms over Hester, Pearl, and Dimmesdale if they reveal Chillingworth's true identity?
4. What does Hester suggest they do?
5. What is Dimmesdale's attitude about life at this point? How does he feel emotionally and physically?

Chapter 18

1. Who have been Hester's teachers in these last seven years, according to the narrator?
2. How has Dimmesdale lived the past seven years?
3. What does Hester do in the middle of the forest that allows the sun to shine on her?
4. How does she feel and look after doing so?
5. Describe Pearl's relationship with nature.

Chapters 16 – 18
Standards Focus: Symbolism

A **symbol** is a representation of an idea, person, or thing by the use of a picture or other object. Oftentimes, a symbol can be a material object which represents an idea or concept that is not physically tangible. For example, a heart is a symbol for love and a light bulb is a symbol for an idea. The use of symbols in literature for a certain image or character is called **symbolism**. Symbols help the reader understand and remember a certain character or part of the story by making the novel deeper in meaning and richer in imagery.

In *The Scarlet Letter,* the rose is a symbol for Hester or Pearl. However, in another book, a rose may be a symbol for another character, or maybe even the idea of blossoming love. It could even unexpectedly symbolize death, depending on the image the author wants the reader to perceive when the object is mentioned. Each piece of literature will use its own set of symbols to represent certain elements of the novel as the author wants the reader to see it. Remember, a symbol is not always something the author deliberately points out or mentions, but it is usually something that must be concluded from evidence given in the text.

Directions: Complete the chart below by writing both what you think the symbol represents and why, and an example from the text of the symbol being mentioned. Be sure to include chapter, page number, and a direct quote from the book to support your answer.

Symbol	What the symbol represents	Support from the text
the scarlet letter	I think the scarlet letter represents punishment in general because it was a punishment for Hester for the rest of her life. Even though she loves Dimmesdale, she committed a sin according to her religion. I also think it symbolizes beauty because Hester embroiders it beautifully and makes it her own, like a representation of who she is inside.	Ch. 2, pg. 49 "so fantastically embroidered and illuminated upon her bosom."
Pearl (and her name)		
the scaffold		

Name _____ Period_____

Symbol	What the symbol represents	Support from the text
the prison		
roses/ rose bush		
Dimmesdale holding his hand over his heart		
the letter *A* in the night sky		

Chapters 16 – 18
Assessment Preparation: Word Origins

Directions: *Using your vocabulary list and a dictionary, find (a) the vocabulary word with the same root as the example, (b) two other words that share the same root, and (c) the definition of the vocabulary word.*

1. The word <u>medium</u> comes from the Latin *medius*, meaning "the middle."

   a. Which vocabulary word has the same root? _____

   b. List two other words that have the same root:

   _____   _____

   c. Definition of the vocabulary word: _____

   _____

2. The word <u>loquacious</u> comes from the Latin *loquitur*, meaning "he/she speaks."

   a. Which vocabulary word has the same root? _____

   b. List two other words that have the same root:

   _____   _____

   c. Definition of the vocabulary word: _____

   _____

3. The word <u>hilly</u> comes from the Old Engilsh *hyllic*, meaning "steep."

   a. Which vocabulary word has the same root? _____

   b. List two other words that have the same root:

   _____   _____

   c. Definition of the vocabulary word: _____

   _____

4. The word <u>consecution</u> comes from the Latin *consecutio*, meaning "to follow."

   a. Which vocabulary word has the same root? _____

   b. List two other words that have the same root:

   _____   _____

   c. Definition of the vocabulary word: _____

   _____

5. The word <u>vestment</u> comes from the Latin *vestigium,* meaning "footprint."

   a. Which vocabulary word has the same root? _____

   b. List two other words that have the same root:

   _____   _____

    c. Definition of the vocabulary word: _____

_____

6. The word <u>collusion</u> comes from the Latin *collude*, meaning "to play together."

    a. Which vocabulary word has the same root? _____

    b. List two other words that have the same root:

    _____   _____

    c. Definition of the vocabulary word: _____

_____

7. The word <u>harried</u> comes from the Middle English *heri*, meaning "to harass."

    a. Which vocabulary word has the same root? _____

    b. List two other words that have the same root:

    _____   _____

    c. Definition of the vocabulary word: _____

_____

8. The word <u>transmission</u> comes from the Latin *transmissus*, meaning "to send across."

    a. Which vocabulary word has the same root? _____

    b. List two other words that have the same root:

    _____   _____

    c. Definition of the vocabulary word: _____

_____

9. The word <u>denigrate</u> comes from the Latin *de nigrare*, meaning "to blacken."

    a. Which vocabulary word has the same root? _____

    b. List two other words that have the same root:

    _____   _____

    c. Definition of the vocabulary word: _____

_____

10. The word <u>dryas</u> comes from the Greek mythology *dryus*, meaning "wood nymph."

    a. Which vocabulary word has the same root? _____

    b. List two other words that have the same root:

    _____   _____

    c. Definition of the vocabulary word: _____

_____

Chapters 19 – 21
Active Reading Guide

Directions: As you read Chapters 19-21 of ***The Scarlet Letter***, examine each character's motivation and actions, completing the chart below. For help, refer to page 25.

	Prynne	**Dimmesdale**	**Chillingworth**
Plot Points			
Motivation			
Prediction			
Connection			
Questions			

Chapters 19 – 21
Comprehension Check

Directions: *As you read each chapter, answer the following questions on a separate piece of paper using complete sentences.*

Chapter 19

1. Why does Pearl hesitate to return to her mother when she is called?
2. What does Pearl want Hester to do before she comes back to her?
3. Describe Pearl's actions upon returning to her mother.
4. What does Hester tell Pearl about Dimmesdale?
5. What does Pearl do after Dimmesdale kisses her? Why do you think she does this?

Chapter 20

1. What have Hester and Dimmesdale decided to do about their situation?
2. As Dimmesdale walks back through town, who does he encounter? What does Dimmesdale do or get the urge to do to each person? Why do you think Dimmesdale feels this way? Explain.
3. What does Mistress Hibbins tell Dimmesdale?
4. What does Dimmesdale tell Chillingworth when he gets back home?
5. What does Dimmesdale do that evening and all through the night?

Chapter 21

1. Describe Election Day and how it is celebrated.
2. What does Pearl ask Hester about Dimmesdale?
3. What observation does Pearl make about Dimmesdale's interaction with them?
4. What news does Hester receive just before the procession starts?
5. Who is staring and smiling at her ominously?

Chapters 19 – 21
Standards Focus: Plot

Plot is one of the most important elements in a novel because it takes part in defining the characters, moving the story from one event to another, and providing structure. The plot is the series of planned events of a literary work and consists of structured points that can be tracked throughout a story. On a basic level, all novels have a beginning, a middle, and an end, no matter how experimental or strange a story might seem. However, there are five other major breakdowns of a plot know as a story arc. A **story arc** is made up of the *starting action, rising action, climax, falling action,* and *dénouement* (also called the *resolution*).

Starting action or **incident** is what gets the plot going; it is the first action that requires a response and therefore, sets the story in motion. In most cases, there is a lot of writing that comes before the starting action, known as the exposition. **Exposition** is the information that the reader needs to know in order to get to know the characters and previous action before the action of the story begins. However, in some cases, the story begins in the middle of the starting action and the exposition is given during or after the action is done. This technique, used in *The Scarlet Letter*, is called **in medias res**.

Rising action involves everything that happens in preparation for the most important part of the story (the climax), and includes the obstacles that the protagonist must overcome to reach his/her goal. All the actions and events in the story that lead to a major change or event are considered part of rising action. It may sometimes be difficult to track rising action because it may not seem like the story is leading to anything exciting. In other cases, the rising action is full of suspense and growing anticipation for the major turning point of the plot.

The **climax** of the story, the most exciting and important part of the plot, determines what will happen to the characters from that point on. The climax is the junction in the story that the author uses to reveal something important or make a major change in how the characters interact. This can sometimes be confusing because there may be more than one major action that can be considered the climax to the story. However, the true climax is the point at which the height of tension takes place, or the moment in which the protagonist makes the most significant change.

Falling action is what happens after the main event, or climax, of the story. What the characters do, how they react, and how the world of the novel changes after the climax is over are all part of the falling action. Oftentimes, the falling action is short and consists of only a quick update of the characters' status since the climax.

Finally, there is the **dénouement** (day-nu-mah), or the resolution. This is where all the loose ends of the story are tied up and the audience finds out what happened to the characters and their circumstances. All final actions of the novel take place and sometimes the reader is given closure about the characters and their stories.

Chapters 19 – 21
Standards Focus: Plot Activity

Directions: Identify the point in **The Scarlet Letter** in which each of the parts of the plot take place. Include the chapter, page number, a brief quotation from the novel, and an explanation of the event. Insert as many examples as you can find to prove what you believe is the starting action, rising action, climax, and falling action. Since you have not finished reading the novel yet, make a prediction as to what you think will happen in the dénouement. Once you have finished reading the novel, revisit this page to see how accurate your prediction was.

Story Arc	*The Scarlet Letter* Citation
Starting Action (Exposition)	Ex. Hester had an affair, became pregnant, and had a child Ch.1, pg. 48: "When the young woman—the mother of this child—stood fully revealed before the crowd…"
Rising Action	
Climax	
Falling Action	
Your Prediction of the Dénouement (Resolution)	

Chapters 19 – 21
Assessment Preparation: Word Parts

Directions: *Complete the following chart. Use a dictionary for help. A sample has been done for you.*

Word	prattle	preternatural	vicissitude	disquietude	uncouth
Base	prattle (similar to prate)				
Meaning of Base	to talk excessively				
Root and Meaning of Root	ME: *praten*; to chatter				
Affix(es) (Prefix or Suffix)	none				
How the Affix Changes the Word	N/A				
Inferred Meaning of Vocabulary Word	to babble; to talk excessively without a point				
Vocabulary Word's Part of Speech and Dictionary Definition	verb; to talk in a simple-minded or foolish way; chatter; babble				

Name _____ Period_____

Word	potentate	obeisance	languor	jocularity	depredation
Base					
Meaning of Base					
Root and Meaning of Root					
Affix(es) (Prefix or Suffix)					
How the Affix Changes the Word					
Inferred Meaning of Vocabulary Word					
Vocabulary Word's Part of Speech and Dictionary Definition					

Chapters 22 – 24
Active Reading Guide

Directions: As you read Chapters 22-24 of **The Scarlet Letter**, examine each character's motivation and actions, completing the chart below. For help, refer to page 25.

	Prynne	Dimmesdale	Chillingworth
Plot Points			
Motivation			
Connection			
Questions			

Chapters 22 – 24
Comprehension Check

Directions: *As you read each chapter, answer the following questions on a separate piece of paper using complete sentences.*

Chapter 22

1. How has Dimmesdale's appearance changed?
2. Describe the verbal interaction between Mistress Hibbins and Hester. What does Hibbons tell Pearl?
3. Where does Hester stand to listen to the sermon? Why?
4. What news does Hester receive during the sermon?
5. What does Hester realize while she is standing by the scaffold?

Chapter 23

1. What do the townspeople say about Dimmesdale's sermon?
2. What does Dimmesdale do instead of following the procession out? What happens?
3. What is Chillingworth's reaction to the scene?
4. What does Pearl do right before Dimmesdale dies? What happens as a result?
5. How do the townspeople initially react to what they witness?

Chapter 24

1. After a few days, what are the townspeople's different reactions to the scene that took place on Election Day?
2. What does Chillingworth do for Pearl after he dies?
3. What do Pearl and Hester do after Chillingworth dies?
4. Why does Hester come back to her cottage after being away for so long?
5. What becomes her new role in the community?
6. What do people assume happened to Pearl? What clues prove this?
7. Where is Hester buried?
8. What is significant about how she is buried in relation to her former lover?

Name _____ Period_____

Chapters 22 – 24
Standards Focus: Theme

The **theme** of a novel is the main idea or lesson that is being taught by the story. In any novel, there may be more than one theme and any of those themes may be a complex concept. Simply put, a theme is a concept or idea that the author wants to explore over the course of the story, and through the story the author's view on that concept or idea is reflected. A theme is an idea that can be discussed, agreed and disagreed upon, and analyzed.

For example, one of the themes of *Lord of the Flies* is **the loss of innocence.** Mary Shelley's *Frankenstein* explores how **science can be dangerous**.

Directions: *For each theme listed, write whether you agree or disagree that this is the point that Hawthorne was trying to make, and why you feel that way. In the next box, show proof from the novel that supports your opinion about the theme. So, for example, if you disagree that Hawthorne believed that evil exists in all people, explain why you think this way and be sure to show proof of your take on the theme with evidence from the text. In the last box, cite proof of any motifs or symbols that support your opinion.*

Theme	Agree or Disagree? Why?	Textual Evidence	Motifs or Symbols
Repressed sin destroys the soul.			
Evil exists in all people.			
A person's identity is partially made up by the society in which he/she lives and by those who govern it.			

Chapters 22 – 24

Assessment Preparation: Connotation and Denotation

Directions*: On the first line, write the definition (denotation) of the vocabulary word. On the second line, write three synonyms for the vocabulary word. Then, write a sentence using the vocabulary word and replace the word with its synonyms using the same sentence. On the last line, write which of the four words has the <u>most powerful</u> connotation to you and why you feel this way. See page 48 for a review if needed.*

1. contiguous

Denotation: _____

_____

Synonyms: _____

Sentences: _____

_____

_____

_____

Most Powerful Connotation: _____

_____

2. gait

Denotation: _____

_____

Synonyms: _____

Sentences: _____

_____

_____

_____

Most Powerful Connotation: _____

_____

3. necromancy

Denotation: _____

_____

Synonyms: _____

Sentences: _____

_____

_____

_____

Name _____ Period_____

Most Powerful Connotation: _____

_____

4. pathos

Denotation: _____

_____

Synonyms: _____

Sentences: _____

_____

_____

_____

Most Powerful Connotation: _____

_____

5. erratic

Denotation: _____

_____

Synonyms: _____

Sentences: _____

_____

_____

_____

Most Powerful Connotation: _____

_____

6. indefatigable

Denotation: _____

_____

Synonyms: _____

Sentences: _____

_____

_____

_____

Most Powerful Connotation: _____

_____

7. audacity

Denotation: _____

_____

Synonyms: _____

Sentences: _____

_____

_____

_____

Most Powerful Connotation: _____

_____

8. repugnance

Denotation: _____

_____

Synonyms: _____

Sentences: _____

_____

_____

_____

Most Powerful Connotation: _____

_____

9. apotheosize

Denotation: _____

_____

Synonyms: _____

Sentences: _____

_____

_____

_____

Most Powerful Connotation: _____

_____

Name _____ Period_____

The Scarlet Letter
Quiz: Chapters 1 – 3

Directions: *On the lines provided, write the name of the character being quoted. Answers may be used more than once and not all answers will be used.*

Hester Prynne   Roger Chillingworth   Mistress Hibbins   Governor Bellingham
the Narrator   Arthur Dimmesdale   Reverend Wilson   woman in the crowd

1. _____ "Ah, but let her cover the mark as she will, the pang of it will always be in her heart."

2. _____ "She will not speak! Wondrous strength and generosity of a woman's heart! She will not speak!"

3. _____ "I am a stranger, and have been a wanderer, sorely against my will. I have met with grievous mishaps by sea and land, and have been long held in bonds among the heathen-folk, to the southward, and am now brought hither by this Indian, to be redeemed out of my captivity."

4. _____ "It may serve, let us hope, to symbolize some sweet moral blossom, that may be found along the track, or relieve the darkening close of the tale of human frailty and sorrow."

5. _____ "I will not speak! And my child must seek a heavenly Father; she shall never know an earthly one!"

6. _____ "Although, by a seemingly careless arrangement of his heterogeneous garb, he had endeavored to conceal or abate the peculiarity, it was sufficiently evident to Hester Prynne that one of this man's shoulders rose higher than the other."

7. _____ "Speak to the woman, my brother. It is of moment to her soul, and therefore, as the worshipful Governor says, momentous to thine own, in whose charge hers is. Exhort her to confess the truth!"

Directions: *For each definition, fill in the **vocabulary word** and **part of speech** on the lines provided.*

inauspicious   physiognomy   beadle   pillory   mien
ignominy   contumely   sagacity   vie   remonstrance

8. _____ _____ to strive in competition for; contend for superiority

9. _____ _____ soundness of judgment; wisdom; mental sharpness

10. _____ _____ boding ill; unfavorable

11. _____ _____ a wooden framework erected on a post, with holes for securing the hands and head in order to expose a criminal to public ridicule or abuse

12. _____ _____ insulting display of contempt in words or action; an insult

13. _____ _____ the face or countenance; the outward appearance

14. _____ _____ a minor church official who ushers or helps preserve order during services

The Scarlet Letter
Quiz: Chapters 1 – 3

15. _____ _____ disgrace; dishonor; shame

16. _____ _____ complaint; objection; protest

17. _____ _____ the look of something; carriage; appearance

Directions: Complete the following, using complete sentences.

18. In a few sentences, describe the Puritan way of life and its system of punishment. _____

_____

_____

_____

_____

_____

_____

_____

_____

19. Explain exactly why and how Hester Prynne is being punished. _____

_____

_____

_____

_____

_____

_____

20. Describe Hester Prynne's state of mind. How has she decided she and Pearl will live their lives?

_____

_____

_____

_____

_____

_____

_____

Name _____ Period_____

The Scarlet Letter
Quiz: Chapters 4 – 6

Directions: *On the line in front of each statement given, write* **True** *if the statement is true or* **False** *if the statement is false.* <u>Write out</u> *the entire word "true" or "false." Then on the lines below the statement, change the false statements into true statements. Do not use the word "not," or just negate the statement. Your rewritten statement should explain how the statement is false.*

1. _____ Hester reveals the name of her lover to Chillingworth, but makes him promise not to tell anyone. _____

_____

2. _____ Chillingworth makes Hester promise to keep his true identity a secret. _____

_____

3. _____ Hester is a bold woman who does not care what people think about her. _____

_____

4. _____ Hester feels that her daughter is her only treasure. _____

_____

5. _____ Hester lives a very happy and fulfilling life with her daughter. _____

_____

6. _____ While Chillingworth visits Hester in jail, he attempts to poison her and her baby. _____

_____

7. _____ Hester supports herself and her child by growing food in her garden and selling it in the market place. _____

_____

8. _____ Chillingworth vows to find out who is Hester's lover. _____

_____

9. _____ Some were afraid that Hester might hurt herself or her child while in prison. _____

_____

10. _____ Hester once loved Chillingworth, but fell out of love with him when he was gone. _____

_____

Directions: *Fill in the* **vocabulary word** *and* **part of speech** *on the lines provided.*

| draught | efficacy | quaff | phantasmagoric | expostulation |
| paramour | uncongenial | sable | gesticulation | anathemas |

11. _____ _____ an animated gesture; a gesture made with excitement

12. _____ _____ disagreeable; not pleasing

13. _____ _____ curses; denunciations; bad wishes

The Scarlet Letter
Quiz: Chapters 4 – 6

14. _____ _____ a drink; a dose; that which is taken by drinking or inhaling

15. _____ _____ displaying an optical illusion; imagining changing scenes

16. _____ _____ effectiveness; able to produce a result

17. _____ _____ complaint; earnest protest

18. _____ _____ to drink heartily

19. _____ _____ black clothes worn in mourning

20. _____ _____ lover; a beloved person

Directions: *Answer the multiple choice questions below by writing the letter of the correct answer on the line provided.*

21. _____ Which of the following quotes BEST reveals that Chillingworth vows to find the man with whom Hester had an affair?
   a. "Wouldst thou avenge thyself on the innocent babe?"
   b. "Drink it! It may be less soothing than a sinless conscience. That I cannot give thee."
   c. "He bears no letter of infamy, wrought into his garment, as thou dost; but I shall read it in his heart."
   d. "Thou hast kept the secret of thy paramour. Keep, likewise, mine!"

22. _____ When Hester is released from jail, where does she go to live?
   a. back to her old home in the Puritan village
   b. to a small abandoned cottage on the outskirts of the town
   c. to stay with a family member in a neighboring town
   d. with Mistress Hibbins, the only person who accepts her and her daughter

23. _____ Why doesn't Hester go back to her home in England?
   a. she is afraid she will not be accepted
   b. she doesn't have any money to go back
   c. she doesn't want to leave her lover
   d. she does not feel sorry for her sin

24. _____ How does Hester make money to support herself and her daughter?
   a. she grows and sells food
   b. she works at the church
   c. she is a translator for the Indians
   d. she embroiders clothes

25. _____ What does Hester sometimes think about Pearl?
   a. that she looks just like her father
   b. that she is a very obedient child
   c. that she looks like a little elf
   d. that she acts like her former husband

Name _____ Period_____

The Scarlet Letter
Quiz: Chapters 7 – 9

Directions: *Fill in the sentences below by writing the correct answer on the line.*

1. Although Hester has to deliver a pair of gloves to _____'s house, the true

   reason she is delivering the gloves personally is that she wants a chance to talk with him.

2. Hester has heard rumors in town that the _____ are considering taking

   _____ away from Hester and letting another family raise her.

3. When the Reverend asks Pearl who made her, she responds by saying that she was not made

   at all, but _____ by her mother off the rose bush that grows in front of the _____.

4. _____ comes to Hester's rescue and defends her, which eventually leads to

   the decision to let her raise her own daughter.

5. As Hester and Pearl leave the house, _____ asks if Hester wants to go meet

   the Black Man in the forest that night.

Directions: *For each definition, fill in the **vocabulary word** and **part of speech** on the lines provided.*

imperious	pestilence	cabalistic	contagion	chirurgical
despondent	deportment	leech	erudition	emaciated

6. _____ _____ surgical; a part of surgery

7. _____ _____ demeanor; conduct; behavior

8. _____ _____ a deadly epidemic or disease; something harmful or evil

9. _____ _____ dictatorial; urgent; commanding

10. _____ _____ knowledge acquired by study; learning; scholarship

11. _____ _____ abnormally thin; marked by lack of nutrition or disease

12. _____ _____ mystic; occult

13. _____ _____ discouraged; feeling or showing no hope

14. _____ _____ parasite; name for a doctor in the 1600's; something that

   clings to another for personal gain

15. _____ _____ the transmission or spread of an attitude, idea, emotion or

   disease; harmful or undesired contact or influence

The Scarlet Letter
Quiz: Chapters 7 – 9

Directions: *Answer the following questions using complete sentences.*

16. What role in the community does Chillingworth take on? What kind of training or schooling has Chillingworth had that qualifies him to take that role?_____

_____

_____

_____

_____

17. How do the townspeople feel about Dimmesdale? _____

_____

_____

_____

18. How do Chillingworth and Dimmesdale end up living together? _____

_____

_____

_____

_____

19. What does the window at Chillingworth and Dimmesdale's home overlook? How might this be symbolic? Explain._____

_____

_____

_____

_____

20. What physical changes is Chillingworth going through? _____

_____

_____

_____

_____

Name _____ Period_____

The Scarlet Letter
Quiz: Chapters 10 – 12

*Directions: On the lines provided below, write whether the speaker of the quote was **Chillingworth** or **Dimmesdale**.*

1. _____ "They grew out of his heart, and typify, it may be, some hideous secret that was buried with him, and which he has done better to confess during his lifetime."

2. _____ "A sickness, a sore place, if we may call it, in your spirit, hath immediately its appropriate manifestation in your bodily frame."

3. _____ "Surely, it were child's play to call in a physician, and then hide the sore!"

4. _____ "There goes a woman who, be her demerits what they may, hath none of that mystery of hidden sinfulness which you deem so grievous to be borne."

5. _____ "So, to their own unutterable torment, they go about among their fellow-creatures, looking pure as new-fallen snow; while their hearts are all speckled and spotted with iniquity of which they cannot rid themselves."

6. _____ "It is as well, to have made this step. There is nothing lost. We shall be friends again anon."

7. _____ "Let him do with me as, in his justice and wisdom, he shall see good."

Directions: Put the events listed below in chronological order. Write the numbers 1-8 on the line in front of the events in the order in which they occurred—the first event being #1, the last, #8.

8. _____ Dimmesdale stands on the scaffold and screams.

9. _____ The letter *A* flashes through the night sky.

10. _____ A churchgoer gives Dimmesdale a black glove found on the scaffold.

11. _____ Chillingworth tries to get Dimmesdale to tell his secret.

12. _____ Pearl asks Dimmesdale to stand with her and Hester at noontide.

13. _____ Chillingworth sees Dimmesdale's secret by looking "into" his heart while Dimmesdale sleeps.

14. _____ Dimmesdale finds out Governor Winthrop has died.

15. _____ Dimmesdale and Chillingworth get into an argument.

The Scarlet Letter
Quiz: Chapters 10 – 12

Directions: *For each definition given, fill in the **vocabulary word** and **part of speech** on the lines.*

ominous	inimical	demerits	ethereal	inextricable
expiation	zenith	somnambulism	scurrilous	portent

16. _____ _____ punishments for bad behavior

17. _____ _____ light; airy; refined; extremely delicate

18. _____ _____ obscenely abusive; insulting; offensive; vulgar

19. _____ _____ foreboding; threatening

20. _____ _____ the highest point; the point in the sky directly above the observer

21. _____ _____ harmful; hostile; unfriendly

22. _____ _____ ominous significance; an indication or omen of something momentous that is about to happen

23. _____ _____ sleepwalking; performing acts while sleeping

24. _____ _____ incapable of being disentangled; hopelessly intricate or involved; unable to be undone or solved

25. _____ _____ the means by which reparation or atonement is made

Name _____ Period_____

The Scarlet Letter
Quiz: Chapters 13 – 15

*Directions: On the line in front of each statement given, write **True** if the statement is true or **False** if the statement is false. Write out the entire word "true" or "false." Then on the lines below the statement, change the false statements into true statements. Do not use the word "not," or just negate the statement. Your rewritten statement should explain how the statement is false.*

1. _____ After the incident on the scaffold in the middle of the night, Hester becomes increasingly worried about Dimmesdale and resolves to tell him Chillingworth's true identity.

_____

_____

2. _____ To the townspeople in Hester's community, the scarlet letter has taken on new meaning. They now believe the A stands for Abominable. _____

_____

3. _____ Hester has a more rebellious personality now than before receiving the scarlet letter. _____

_____

4. _____ Chillingworth's appearance has become softer and more handsome over the course of the novel. _____

_____

5. _____ When Hester and Chillingworth meet in the forest, they have a pleasant conversation in which they decide to come clean to society about each of their secrets. ___

_____

_____

6. _____ While Hester talks to Chillingworth, Pearl is playing with seaweed by the seashore, fashioning the letter P to put on her chest. _____

_____

7. _____ Pearl makes a connection between the scarlet letter and Dimmesdale. _____

_____

8. _____ Hester is tempted to tell Pearl all about her suffering and the truth about the scarlet letter. _____

_____

9. _____ When Pearl asks about why Hester wears the *A* on her chest, Hester is honest and tells her the truth. _____

_____

10. _____ By the end of Chapter 15, it has been 10 years since Hester received the scarlet letter. _____

*Directions: For each definition given, fill in the **vocabulary word** and **part of speech** on the lines.*

gibe	innate	austerity	effluence	proffered
petulant	requital	enigma	asperity	despotic

11. _____ _____ offered or proposed for one's acceptance or rejection

12. _____ _____ a return or reward for service; kindness

13. _____ _____ holding absolute power; tyrannical

The Scarlet Letter
Quiz: Chapters 13 – 15

14. _____ _____ severity of manner or tone; harshness; roughness

15. _____ _____ existing in one from birth; inborn; not learned

16. _____ _____ something that flows out; outward expression

17. _____ _____ mocking words; taunts

18. _____ _____ showing sudden impatience or irritation

19. _____ _____ stern coldness in appearance and manner; without excess or ornamentation

20. _____ _____ a person of contradicting or puzzling character; riddle; problem

Directions: *Answer the following questions using complete sentences.*

21. In what ways has Hester changed over the years since receiving the scarlet letter? _____

_____

_____

_____

_____

22. What do the townspeople now think of Hester? _____

_____

_____

23. How does this compare to their own thoughts on the first day of her punishment? _____

_____

_____

_____

24. Why does Hester resolve to tell Dimmesdale the truth about Chillingworth's identity?_____

_____

_____

_____

_____

25. What is important about the response that Hester gives when Pearl asks what the scarlet letter means? _____

_____

_____

_____

_____

Name _____ Period_____

The Scarlet Letter
Quiz: Chapters 16 – 18

Directions: Answer the multiple choice questions below by writing the letter of the best answer on the line provided.

_____ 1. What does Pearl say is the reason the sun does not shine on her mother?
      a. the sun is afraid of the scarlet letter   c. it is night time
      b. the sun only shines on children   d. God has forsaken her

_____ 2. When Hester and Pearl sit down to take a rest in the forest, Pearl wants to hear a story about what?
      a. the Black Man   c. Jesus
      b. other children   d. her father

_____ 3. What is Dimmesdale's initial reaction when Hester reveals the truth about Chillingworth?
      a. happy and relieved   c. angry and in despair
      b. shocked but pleased   d. happy but worried

_____ 4. What happens when Hester takes off her cap and the scarlet letter?
      a. it begins to rain   c. Pearl screams
      b. Dimmesdale kisses her   d. sunshine falls upon her

_____ 5. How does Hester feel after taking off the letter and letting her hair fall freely?
      a. like a weight has been lifted from her   c. scared
      b. worried that someone will see her   d. nervous

Directions: For each definition given, fill in the **vocabulary word** and **part of speech** on the lines.

| meditative | loquacity | hillock | consecration | vestige |
| colloquy | harrowed | dryad | transmuting | denizen |

6. _____ _____ an inhabitant; resident

7. _____ _____ a dialogue; conversation; conference

8. _____ _____ a deity or nymph of the woods

9. _____ _____ deeply thoughtful; contemplative

10. _____ _____ a little hill

11. _____ _____ changing from one form to another; transforming

12. _____ _____ visible evidence of something that is no longer present; a mark or trace

13. _____ _____ talkativeness; chattiness

14. _____ _____ the act of giving sacramental character; sacredness

15. _____ _____ distressed the mind; disturbed keenly or painfully

The Scarlet Letter
Quiz: Chapters 16 – 18

Directions: *Answer the following questions using complete sentences.*

16. What does Pearl think will happen to her when she is grown? _____

_____

_____

17. What does Hester tell Pearl about meeting the Black Man? _____

_____

_____

_____

18. What is the constant reminder that Dimmesdale is suffering? _____

_____

_____

_____

19. Why does the reverence of Dimmesdale's parishioners towards him make him feel even worse about himself? _____

_____

_____

_____

20. What is Pearl's relationship with nature? Explain. _____

_____

_____

_____

_____

_____

Name _____ Period_____

The Scarlet Letter
Quiz: Chapters 19 – 21

Directions: *On the lines provided, write the name of the character that best matches the quote given. Answers may be used more than once, and not all answers will be used.*

Pearl	a sailor	Narrator	Hester	Rev. Wilson
Dimmesdale	Chillingworth	Mistress Hibbins	Governor Bellingham	

1. _____ "At least, they shall say of me that I leave no public duty unperformed, nor ill performed."

2. _____ "Dost thou know, Hester, that this dear child, tripping about always at thy side, hath caused me many an alarm?"

3. _____ "We will have a home and fireside of our own; and thou shalt sit upon his knee; and he will teach thee many things, and love thee dearly."

4. _____ "I must bid the steward make ready one more berth than you bargained for! No fear of scurvy or ship-fever this voyage!"

5. _____ "So, Reverend Sir, you have made a visit to the forest. The next time, I pray you to allow me only fair warning and I shall be proud to bear you company."

6. _____ "For some unaccountable reason, as Arthur Dimmesdale felt the child's eyes upon himself, his hand—with that gesture so habitual as to have become involuntary—stole over his heart."

7. _____ "Our Pearl is a fitful and fantastic little elf sometimes."

Directions: *For each definition given, fill in the **vocabulary word** and **part of speech** on the lines.*

prattle	preternatural	vicissitude	disquietude	uncouth
potentate	languor	obeisance	jocularity	depredation

8. _____ _____ physical weakness; lack of energy; sluggish; lack of spirit

9. _____ _____ rude; uncivilized; unmannerly; of ungraceful appearance

10. _____ _____ the act of preying upon or plundering; robbery

11. _____ _____ to talk in a simple-minded or foolish way; babble

12. _____ _____ state or quality of being facetious or joking; a funny remark

13. _____ _____ out of the ordinary; unnatural

14. _____ _____ power; ruler; monarch

15. _____ _____ a change or variation in the course of something; unexpected change

16. _____ _____ a bow or curtsey; a movement of the body expressing respect

17. _____ _____ the state of disturbance; uneasiness; noisiness

The Scarlet Letter
Quiz: Chapters 22 – 24

Directions: Put the events listed below in chronological order. Write the numbers 1-10 on the line in front of the events in the order in which they occurred—the first event being #1, the last, #10.

1. _____ Pearl inherits a fortune.

2. _____ Dimmesdale dies.

3. _____ Hester receives news that Chillingworth will be joining her and Dimmesdale on their escape to Bristol.

4. _____ Hester dies and is buried next to Dimmesdale.

5. _____ Hester and Pearl go back to England.

6. _____ Dimmesdale gives the Election Day sermon.

7. _____ Hester comes back to her cottage in New England.

8. _____ Dimmesdale confesses his sin upon the scaffold.

9. _____ Chillingworth dies.

10. _____ Mistress Hibbons says Pearl is the daughter of the Prince of the Air.

Directions: For each definition given, fill in the **vocabulary word** and **part of speech** on the lines.

contiguous	morion	gait	necromancy	pathos
erratic	indefatigable	audacity	repugnance	apotheosize

11. _____ _____ the art of divination through communication with the dead

12. _____ _____ incapable of being tired out; not tiring

13. _____ _____ glorify; deify

14. _____ _____ deviating from the proper or usual course in conduct or opinion

15. _____ _____ in close proximity with; close by; touching

16. _____ _____ strong distaste or aversion; objection

17. _____ _____ a manner of walking, stepping, or running

18. _____ _____ the quality or power of evoking pity or compassion

19. _____ _____ daring without regard for personal safety; boldness

20. _____ _____ helmet worn by common soldiers in the 16th and 17th centuries

The Scarlet Letter
Quiz: Chapters 22 – 24

Directions: Answer the questions below using complete sentences.

21. What happens upon the scaffold (after Dimmesdale confesses his sin) that changes Pearl's life? Explain why this is important. _____

_____

_____

_____

_____

_____

22. Why does Hester come back to her old cottage in New England after being away for such a long time? _____

_____

_____

_____

_____

23. What evidence do the townspeople see that proves that Pearl is grown and even has a child?

_____

_____

_____

_____

_____

24. After Hester returns to her cottage, she takes on a new role in the community. What is this new role and what is significant about it? _____

_____

_____

_____

_____

25. What is important about where and how Hester is buried? _____

_____

_____

_____

_____

Name _____ Period_____

The Scarlet Letter
Final Exam

Part A: Identification
Directions: On the line at the left, write the name of the character who best fits the description, OR if it is a quote from the novel, write the name of the character who spoke the words. Answers may be used more than once.

1._____ "Come away, or yonder old Black Man will catch you! He hath got hold of the minister already."

2._____ forced to be publicly humiliated for three hours

3._____ "What little bird of scarlet plumage may this be?"

4._____ "Thou hast escaped me! Thou hast escaped me!"

5._____ "Thou wast not bold! Thou wast not true! Thou wouldst not promise to take my hand… tomorrow noontide!"

6._____ "Were I worthy to be quit of it, it would fall away of its own nature, or be transformed into something that should speak a different purport."

7._____ keeps his hand over his heart

8._____ accused of being a witch and later hanged for it

9._____ the product of an illicit love affair

10._____ held captive by Native Americans

Part B: True/False
Directions: Write "**True**" if the statement is true, or "**False**" if the statement is false. Be sure to <u>write out</u> the entire word true or false so there is no confusion about your answer.

11._____ Before arriving to New England, Hester Prynne was married.

12._____ Arthur Dimmesdale is the governor of New England.

13._____ Hester names her child Pearl because of her beautifully round and soft face.

14._____ After being charged with adultery, Hester and Pearl go back to England.

15._____ Hester and Chillingworth are about the same age.

16._____ The Reverend keeps his hand over his heart because he is in constant agony and physical pain.

17._____ Over time, the people in Hester's community begin to like and respect her.

18._____ When Hester and Dimmesdale meet in the forest, they decide to run away to another community in New England.

19._____ Hester goes back to England and helps Pearl raise her own child.

20._____ When Hester returns to her cottage at the end of the story, she no longer wears the scarlet letter.

Name _____ Period_____

Part C: Multiple Choice
Directions: Write the letter of the best choice in the line provided.

_____ 21. Who is the protagonist of the novel?
   a. Hester Prynne   c. Roger Chillingworth
   b. Pearl   d. Mistress Hibbins

_____ 22. What is the technique that Hawthorne uses to begin *The Scarlet Letter*?
   a. setting   c. in medias res
   b. motif   d. symbolism

_____ 23. Mistress Hibbins is a _____ character.
   a. flat   c. round
   b. dynamic   d. protagonist

_____ 24. The Reverend's hand over his heart throughout the novel is a motif that BEST
             supports which theme?
   a. love conquers all   c. there is humanity in all people
   b. secret sin can be fatal   d. none of these

_____ 25. What is the setting of the novel?
   a. Bristol, England   c. a New England colony
   b. The Spanish Main   d. early New York City

_____ 26. What is the climax of the novel?
   a. Hester and Dimmesdale meeting in the forest
   b. Hester is placed on the scaffold to receive her punishment
   c. Pearl asks her mother what the scarlet letter means
   d. Dimmesdale confessing his sin in front of the townspeople

_____ 27. What is/are the main conflict(s) of this story?
   a. the people of the colony trying to live through the winter
   b. Chillingworth trying to torture Dimmesdale, who is in constant agony
   c. Hester and Dimmesdale trying to live their lives after committing a sin
   d. both b and c

_____ 28. What is the starting action, or incident, that opens the novel?
   a. Chillingworth arrives in town   c. Dimmesdale gives a good sermon
   b. Hester is on trial for her crime d. Hester is being punished for her crime

_____ 29. The scaffold is MOST likely a symbol of which of the following?
   a. freedom   c. justice
   b. punishment   d. love

_____ 30. Which of the following words best describe Puritan society?
   a. rigid   c. understanding
   b. strict   d. both a and b

_____ 31. What does the rose symbolize in this novel?
   a. Pearl   c. nature
   b. beauty   d. all of the above

_____ 32. What is a theme?
- a. the main idea, or lesson being taught in the story
- b. a prominent image that recurs throughout the novel
- c. a way to keep track of the development of each character in the novel
- d. the main character of the story

_____ 33. What is plot?
- a. the location in which the story takes place
- b. the plan or main story of the novel
- c. a reference to another character or story
- d. the point in the story that is the most intense and important

_____ 34. What type of conflict exists between Dimmesdale and the guilt of his sin?
- a. man vs. man
- b. man vs. self
- c. man vs. nature
- d. none of the above

_____ 35. A character arc is a device that:
- a. allows the reader to track the development of each character
- b. references another character from another story
- c. allows the author to use indirect characterization
- d. tells what each character is a symbol for

Part D: Short Response
Directions*: Answer the following questions in complete sentences. Be sure to include as many details and examples from the text as possible.*

36. What do you think is the main message or theme of this story? What evidence from the story causes you to conclude this? Include specific examples to support your response. _____

_____

_____

_____

_____

_____

_____

_____

_____

37. What do you think that teenagers today can learn from *The Scarlet Letter*? How is the story relevant to today's political and social issues? _____

_____

_____

_____

_____

_____

Name _____ Period_____

_____

_____

_____

Part E: Vocabulary Matching I
Directions: *Match the following vocabulary words with the correct definition. Write the letter of the definition in front of the word on the lines provided.*

_____ 38. inauspicious

a. wisdom; soundness of judgment

_____ 39. sagacity

b. animated gestures

_____ 40. efficacy

c. harmful; hostile; unfriendly

_____ 41. gesticulation

d. effectiveness; producing an effect

_____ 42. pestilence

e. dispirited; feeling or showing hopelessness

_____ 43. despondent

f. showing sudden impatience or irritation

_____ 44. deportment

g. incapable of being disentangled; hopelessly intricate

_____ 45. inimical

h. boding ill; unfavorable

_____ 46. inextricable

i. a deadly epidemic or disease; something evil

_____ 47. petulant

j. demeanor; conduct; behavior

Vocabulary Matching II

_____ 48. enigma

a. pity or compassion

_____ 49. loquacity

b. a person of contradicting or puzzling character; riddle

_____ 50. colloquy

c. a dialogue; conversational exchange; conference

_____ 51. denizen

d. rude; discourteous; awkward

_____ 52. prattle

e. to utter by chattering or babbling

_____ 53. uncouth

f. boldness or daring without regard to safety

_____ 54. languor

g. strong distaste or aversion; objection; revulsion

_____ 55. pathos

h. talkativeness; chattiness; state of talking freely

_____ 56. audacity

i. physical weakness; lack of energy or spirit

_____ 57. repugnance

j. a resident or inhabitant

Name _____ Period_____

The Scarlet Letter
Final Exam- Multiple Choice Version

Part A: Reading
Directions: On your answer sheet, fill in the bubble of the correct response. (If you are **not** using a separate answer sheet, circle the letter of the correct response.)

1. Who is the protagonist of the novel?
   a. Hester Prynne
   b. Roger Chillingworth
   c. Pearl
   d. Mistress Hibbins

2. The first chapter focuses on:
   a. the prison door
   b. the Election Day
   c. Hester
   d. Pearl

3. Hester lives:
   a. in the center of town
   b. on the outskirts of the village
   c. in England
   d. at the church

4. Roger Chillingworth is Hester's:
   a. friend
   b. husband
   c. boyfriend
   d. lover

5. Arthur Dimmesdale is a:
   a. minister
   b. Native American
   c. governor
   d. doctor

6. Hester promises Chillingworth that she will:
   a. tell him the name of her lover
   b. keep his true identity a secret
   c. raise Pearl as a Puritan
   d. leave town

7. Hester makes a living by:
   a. embroidering clothes
   b. growing food in her garden
   c. working in the governor's house
   d. working for the church

8. Throughout the seven years that the novel takes place, the emotion that Hester experiences the most is:
   a. joy
   b. regret
   c. fear
   d. loneliness

9. What does the rose symbolize in this novel?
   a. Pearl
   b. nature
   c. beauty
   d. all of the above

10. Mistress Hibbins is a _____ character.
    a. dynamic
    c. round
    b. flat
    d. protagonist

11. Hester goes to the governor's house to:
    a. ask him to let her raise Pearl
    b. deliver gloves
    c. visit Mistress Hibbins
    d. a and b only

12. Pearl is often described as:
    a. sweet
    b. mean
    c. elfish
    d. funny

13. Hester's only companion is:
    a. Dimmesdale
    b. Mistress Hibbins
    c. Chillingworth
    d. Pearl

14. Dimmesdale holding his hand over his heart throughout the novel is a motif which supports which theme?
    a. love conquers all
    b. there is humanity in all people
    c. secrets can hurt one's soul
    d. none of these

15. What is the climax of the novel?
    a. Dimmesdale confesses his sin in front of the townspeople
    b. Hester and Dimmesdale meet in the forest
    c. Hester is placed on the scaffold to receive her punishment
    d. Pearl asks her mother what the scarlet letter means

16. Chillingworth makes it his mission to _____ Dimmesdale.
   a. cure
   b. help
   c. torment
   d. make enemies with

17. A character arc is a device that:
   a. allows the reader to track the development of each character
   b. references another character from another story
   c. allows the author to use indirect characterization
   d. tells what each character is a symbol for

18. When Dimmesdale confesses his sin on the scaffold, Chillingworth screams:
   a. "Art thou a man?"
   b. "WHY?!"
   c. "He is the sinner!"
   d. "Thou hast escaped me!"

19. What was likely found on Dimmesdale's chest?
   a. a crucifix
   b. an *A*
   c. a heart
   d. a hand print

20. What is the technique that Hawthorne uses to start and introduce the story to the reader?
   a. setting
   b. in medias res
   c. motif
   d. symbolism

21. What flashes through the night sky when Dimmesdale holds one of his nightly vigils?
   a. an eagle
   b. lightning
   c. the letter *A*
   d. a shooting star

22. Which of the following words BEST describes Puritan society?
   a. rigid
   b. individualistic
   c. communal
   d. both a and c

23. The scaffold is most likely a symbol of :
   a. freedom
   b. justice
   c. punishment
   d. hatred

24. What is the setting of the novel?
   a. Bristol, England
   b. a New England colony
   c. The Spanish Main
   d. early New York City

25. How old is Pearl when Dimmesdale finally confesses his sin to the townspeople?
   a. 10
   b. 15
   c. 7
   d. 4

26. As the book progresses, Chillingworth looks more and more like:
   a. the devil
   b. Dimmesdale
   c. his father
   d. a Native American

27. What is/are the main conflict(s) of the story?
   a. the people of the colony trying to survive through the winter
   b. Chillingworth trying to torture Dimmesdale, who is in constant agony
   c. Hester and Dimmesdale trying to live their lives after committing a sin
   d. both b and c

28. What is the starting action, or incident, that opens the novel?
   a. Hester is on trial for her crime
   b. Dimmesdale gives a good sermon
   c. Election Day
   d. Hester is being punished for her crime

29. What type of conflict exists between Dimmesdale and the guilt of his sin?
   a. man vs. man
   b. man vs. nature
   c. man vs. self
   d. none of the above

30. When Pearl asks Hester if she has ever met the Black Man, Hester says:
   a. "No, never."
   b. "Once in my life I met the Black man. This scarlet letter is his mark."
   c. "That is none of thy business."
   d. "You are too young to ask such questions."

31. What is *plot*?
    a. the location in which a story takes place
    b. the plan or main storyline of the novel
    c. a reference to another character or story
    d. the point in the story that is the most intense and important

32. When Hester reveals the true identity of Chillingworth to Dimmesdale, his initial reaction is:
    a. anger and despair
    b. relief and happiness
    c. rage and euphoria
    d. indifference

33. Just before Dimmesdale dies, Pearl:
    a. calls him "Father"
    b. kisses him
    c. screams
    d. apologizes to him

34. What is a *theme*?
    a. the lesson being taught by the story
    b. a prominent image that recurs throughout the novel
    c. a way to keep track of the development of each character in the novel
    d. the main character of the story

35. Hester headstone reads:
    a. "Here lies Hester Prynne: Devoted Mother and Lover of All Things Beautiful"
    b. "Hester Dimmesdale: wife, mother"
    c. "In sooth, in death, thou hast received thy reconciliation"
    d. "On a field, sable, the letter A gules"

Part B: Vocabulary

Directions: *Choose the letter of the correct vocabulary word according to the definitions or synonyms given.*

36. a deadly epidemic or disease
    a. sable   c. pestilence
    b. draught   d. quaff

37. boding ill; unfavorable
    a. inauspicious   c. erudition
    b. phantasmagoric   d. mien

38. utter; chatter; babble
    a. innate   c. austerity
    b. prattle   d. inauspicious

39. showing sudden impatience or irritation
    a. gibe   c. draught
    b. portent   d. petulant

40. a dialogue or conversational exchange
    a. demerits   c. languor
    b. colloquy   d. inimical

41. physical weakness; lack of energy or spirit
    a. languor   c. pathos
    b. expiation   d. meditative

42. incapable of being disentangled; hopelessly intricate
    a. ethereal   c. inextricable
    b. requital   d. dryad

43. pity or compassion
    a. morion   c. pathos
    b. jocularity   d. erratic

44. effectiveness; producing an effect
    a. cabalistic   c. vie
    b. efficacy   d. pillory

45. wisdom; soundness of judgment
    a. quaff   c. beadle
    b. ominous   d. sagacity

46. demeanor; behavior; conduct
    a. deportment   c. despondent
    b. demerits   d. physiognomy

47. an inhabitant or resident
    a. zenith   c. denizen
    b. potentate   d. languor

48. boldness or daring without regard to safety
    a. indefatigable   c. gait
    b. audacity   d. repugnance

49. harmful; hostile; unfriendly
    a. ominous   c. draught
    b. erudition   d. inimical

50. strong distaste or aversion to; objection; revulsion
    a. depredation   c. apotheosize
    b. repugnance   d. jocularity

Teacher Guide
Summary of the Novel

Chapters 1-3

The first chapter of the novel is famously dedicated simply to the description of the prison door and the rose bush in front of it. Chapter 2 goes on to explain that the crowd is gathering in front of the prison door and around the scaffold to witness the punishment of Hester Prynne, the protagonist of the novel, who is holding her newborn baby.

Hester is described as a beautiful woman who, despite being locked up in prison, is still radiant and wears the scarlet letter that is part of her punishment. The women who jeer at Hester are especially harsh and suggest that the letter be branded on her body instead of only being worn on her dress.

As Hester stands on the scaffold facing the crowds, she thinks about her childhood and about her former life before coming to the New World. But as Hester stands embarrassed in front of the crowd, she sees a familiar face belonging to an older man. Seeing that he has been recognized, the man lays a finger over his lips warning Hester to stay quiet about the man's presence.

The man asks another townsperson in the crowd what is happening, and the man explains that Hester is being punished for having committed adultery against her husband who is either on his way from England or has been lost at sea. He also tells the stranger that Hester refuses to give the name of her lover and must therefore suffer the punishment of her crime alone. As Hester stands holding the baby, Governor Bellingham and Reverend Wilson plead for her to reveal the name of her fellow sinner, but Hester refuses to speak it. The men turn to Reverend Arthur Dimmesdale, hoping that since she is one of his congregants he may be able to convince her to give the name of her child's father. Once again though, Hester vows never to reveal his name. Dimmesdale gives up and places his hand over his heart as he steps back from the balcony.

Chapter 4-6

After Hester has finished her time on the scaffold, she returns to the prison where the man she recognized in the crowd comes to visit her. He tells the guard that his name is Roger Chillingworth and that he is a doctor who can help Hester calm down. It is revealed through dialogue that this man is indeed Hester's husband and that he has spent the past year studying the remedies of the Indians and using them in conjunction with his studies in alchemy. He gives Hester and the baby medicine to calm their nerves and then asks that Hester keep his true identity a secret. She promises to do so; while he vows to find the person with whom she shares her sin.

When Hester is released from prison, she moves into an abandoned cottage on the outskirts of the town. She decides not to run away and face life in the wilderness or in another community, but to stay and face the consequences of her actions. To make a living, she embroiders elaborate lace garments for governors, ministers, babies, and even for the dead to wear in their coffins. As time goes on, her scarlet letter becomes more and more adorned with her handiwork and even her beloved daughter Pearl is adorned with the most beautiful clothes and embroidery that her mother can produce. Although Hester is still close to the town and has contact with those she works for, she suffers from severe loneliness and alienation. Every time she goes into the market-place, with Pearl as her only companion, she is subjected to dirty looks and children laughing and calling names behind them. But with this punishment, Hester also gains a gift. She can see into the hearts and eyes of those who look at her and is able to see that they have also sinned. She can see the guilt and feel the shame they feel as she walks by them. This small gift gives Hester some comfort, allowing her to feel that she is not suffering alone in the world.

The next chapter elaborates on Pearl—a strange but beautiful child—around whom Hester's world revolves. She dresses the child in fine clothes and she stands out among nature's beauty. Pearl is a particularly attentive child and she recognizes her mother's loneliness and knows that the scarlet letter on her mother's bosom has some special meaning. She becomes Hester's only companion. However, Pearl often shows strange signs of petulance and says strange things. Hester often wonders if Pearl was not sent to her by the devil as a punishment for her sin and sometimes even calls Pearl an elf or imp-child.

Chapters 7-9
Hester and Pearl arrive at the house of Governor Bellingham, where Hester is delivering a pair of gloves that she has embroidered for him. Hawthorne describes in detail the decorations in the house and especially the suit of armor that adorns his hallway. Hester uses the excuse of the delivery of the gloves to the Governor's house to plead on her own behalf in response to rumors in town that the magistrates are thinking about taking Pearl away from her and giving her to a family that exemplifies more Godly values. She hopes to have the opportunity to talk to the Governor and prove to him that she is a fit mother who is raising Pearl within the proper Puritan standards. When the Governor meets with her, he is accompanied by Wilson, Dimmesdale, and Chillingworth.

Mr. Wilson asks Pearl who made her and instead of answering "God" she replies that she was not made at all, but rather plucked from the rosebush outside the prison. Knowing that this displeases the Governor, Hester pleads for Dimmesdale to fight on her behalf, and thanks to him, the Governor agrees to let Hester raise her own child. On her way out, Hester is approached by Mistress Hibbins who offers to take Hester out to the forest to meet the Black Man. Wisely, Hester refuses and goes home.

The community begins to notice that Dimmesdale is seemingly growing more and more ill. They also believe that Chillingworth, who is disguised as a physician, was sent to them as a gift from God to save their pastor, who always keeps his hand over his heart and has become increasingly emaciated. Chillingworth insists that the best way to diagnose the minister is to be close to him and find a cure for what is ailing him. The two men begin living together and are hardly ever apart. However, as the two become closer, Chillingworth begins to change. His face gets darker and starts to take on an almost evil look. Even the community notices it and wonders if perhaps he was not a gift from God, but rather the devil himself who has come to claim the minister's soul.

Chapters 10-12
Chillingworth and Dimmesdale continue to live together while Chillingworth tries to find out what is ailing the minister. One day, while they are together they begin to discuss sin and buried guilt. All of a sudden from outside of their window they hear laughter. It is Pearl, who is playing in the graveyard below them. Chillingworth brings up Hester and how she openly wears her sin on her chest. Dimmesdale quickly goes on the defensive and becomes upset, then storms out of the room. Not long after, the two make up and are friends once again. One afternoon Chillingworth sees Dimmesdale taking a nap on a chair and becomes curious as to what lies over the heart that the minister is always touching. Gently, Chillingworth pulls away the minister's robes and sees something that makes him immensely happy. The reader is never told what it is, but Chillingworth is overtaken with feelings of joy and ecstasy.

From that point on, Chillingworth focuses all of his attention not on curing the minister, but on exacting a more specific revenge upon him. As Dimmesdale struggles against Chillingworth's psychological torture, he becomes more and more consumed by his sin. He begins holding nightly vigils, staying up all night or staring at his own reflection in a mirror and sometimes even physically punishing himself until his knees buckle. He also fights the urge to stand up in front of the community and confess his sin. One night, the minister decides to confess on the scaffold under the cloak of night.

He climbs to the scaffold and the pain in his chest is so severe that he uncontrollably screams out into the night. Realizing what has just happened, he expects that the whole town will come running out of their houses and see him. But this never happens, and the minister continues to stand there until he sees a light drawing closer to him. It is the Reverend Mr. Wilson who is just making his way home from the deathbed of Governor Winthrop. Words of greeting run through Dimmesdale's brain, but he never actually speaks them aloud and the Reverend simply passes by without noticing Dimmesdale. Dumbfounded by the whole situation, Dimmesdale starts to laugh and is responded to by a laugh in the distance. Slowly Pearl and Hester, who are also coming from Governor Winthrop's house, come into focus. Dimmesdale asks Pearl and Hester to join him on the scaffold and the three of them hold hands, forming an "electric chain." Suddenly, a bright light caused by a meteor flashes across the night sky, making it seem for a moment as if it is the middle of the day. Dimmesdale looks up and sees a bright *A* emblazoned in the sky. As the sky is lit up, Pearl points to Chillingworth, who is standing a few yards away watching the scene. He goes to the minister and tells him that he will accompany him home, as he is also on his way from Winthrop's house. The next day, Dimmesdale is certain that the whole town will know what happened. Instead, most of the town believes that the *A* which gleamed in the night sky was a sign that Governor Winthrop had died and entered Heaven as an angel.

Chapter 13-15
Chapter 13 explains that Hester has changed dramatically since first receiving her scarlet letter. She has since become a valued member of the community, donating her extra time to the poor and needy, and becoming much more calm and reserved. She even looks different, with simpler clothing and her hair always back in a cap. Since her last encounter with Dimmesdale, she has become increasingly worried about his well-being and makes it her mission to try to find a way to protect him from Chillingworth, who she knows is the root of his infirmity.

One day, as Hester is walking along the beach with Pearl, she sees Chillingworth gathering herbs and shrubs, and tells Pearl to go play. Hester begs him to stop torturing Dimmesdale and says that she thinks it is time she tells the minister Chillingworth's true identity. More than ever, Chillingworth is certain that Dimmesdale is Hester's former lover and he is even further transformed into an ugly and evil figure. The conversation ends with Chillingworth saying "It is our fate. Let the black flower blossom as it may!"

Hester calls back Pearl, who has been playing with eel-grass and making a letter like her mother's to place on her own chest. When Hester asks if Pearl understands why she must wear the scarlet letter, Pearl responds "It is for the same reason that the minister keeps his hand over his heart." Pearl has made the connection between the two, but is unsure of what it all means. Hester tells Pearl that she wears it only for the sake of the gold threading.

Chapters 16-18
Knowing that Dimmesdale will be alone in the forest at a certain hour on a specific day, Hester resolves to try to meet him there and tell him the truth about Chillingworth. While they are waiting for the minister to come, Pearl asks her mother if she has ever met the Black Man. Hester confesses that she did once and that the letter she now wears is the mark of their meeting. When Hester catches sight of Dimmesdale, she urges Pearl to go off and play while she talks to him.

Finally, the two are able to talk freely. Hester reveals the truth about Chillingworth, and Dimmesdale is enraged by the confession. He quickly recovers and forgives her, and the two plan their escape. They plot to leave on the ship that is headed back for the Spanish Main in a few days and to go on living as a family. With newfound hope and joy, Dimmesdale and Hester talk of being happy together, away from all who know of them and their sin. In an act to prove that the past is the past, Hester throws off her letter and lets her hair loose from her cap. With a weight having been lifted from her shoulders, Hester becomes excited over the idea of Dimmesdale and Pearl finally getting to know each other. She calls Pearl back to them, and seeing the minister there, Pearl approaches slowly and cautiously.

Chapters 19-21
Once Pearl realizes that her mother is no longer wearing the scarlet letter and her hair is loose, she refuses to come any closer. Hester reluctantly puts the letter back on and gathers her hair, and then Pearl comes to her, kisses her mother and the familiar letter on her bosom. As Hester encourages Pearl to embrace Dimmesdale, Pearl asks if he will go back into the town with them. After Hester tells her no, Dimmesdale kisses Pearl on the forehead. But Pearl does not take kindly to this gesture and runs to the brook to wash off his kiss. She then stands by the water and watches her parents as they finalize their getaway plans.

As Dimmesdale heads back into the town, he is overcome with the desire to say mean things and to perform wicked deeds, such as utter blasphemous suggestions to one of his fellow deacons or utter oaths to the sailors. When he is almost home, he comes across Mistress Hibbins, who offers to go with him the next time he goes into the forest. Disturbed by the observation, Dimmesdale begins to think that he has sold his soul to the Black Man. However, intent on fulfilling all his duties as a clergyman, he hurries home to rewrite his sermon for the Election Day holiday.

For this holiday, all of the townspeople dress up and gather in the town square to wait for the procession. As Hester waits for the procession to hear Dimmesdale's sermon, she gets news from a sailor that Chillingworth will be joining them on their passage to Europe, as he is a doctor and is needed on the ship. She looks up to see Chillingworth's ominous eyes and evil smile.

Chapter 22-24

When the procession begins, Hester, Pearl, and all the townspeople notice how healthy and rejuvenated Dimmesdale looks. Mistress Hibbins approaches Hester and asks her if the minister is the same as when she met him in the forest just a few days before. Shocked, Hester pretends not to know what the old lady is talking about. By this time, the initial prayer has been said and the sermon is about to begin. Hester stands by the foot of the scaffold and listens to Dimmesdale's sermon. Pearl comes to her and delivers a message from the sailor that Chillingworth will indeed be on the ship. As Hester is absorbed in thought about what she has just heard, she comes to realize that the townspeople are staring at her.

As Dimmesdale finishes his sermon, the people reflect that it was his most passionate and sincere sermon yet. As he leaves, he is drawn towards the scaffold, where he sees Hester and Pearl standing. He climbs onto the scaffold and brings the two with him. As Chillingworth catches sight of what is happening, he rushes towards the scaffold and tries to convince Dimmesdale to stop what he is doing. However, Dimmesdale refuses to listen to him and in front of all the people he confesses the sin that has been haunting him for seven years and tears away the clothes from his chest to reveal what is there (once again the narrator does not reveal it). The crowd is dumbfounded, and after saying what he wants to say to the people, Dimmesdale collapses on the scaffold. Chillingworth screams "Thou hast escaped me!" In his last moments, Pearl kisses her father and Hester asks if they will see each other in Heaven. Dimmesdale answers that it is up to God whether they will be further punished for their sin.

Years later, rumors persist about what actually happened on Election Day. Some people say that there was nothing on the minister's chest at all, while others say that he had a scarlet letter like Hester's emblazoned on his flesh. Because Chillingworth no longer had an object of hate and therefore no reason to live, his death came within a year of Dimmesdale's. Upon his death, Chillingworth bequeathed a large amount of property to Pearl, making her the richest heiress in the New World. Soon after his death, both Pearl and Hester vanished and no one heard anything but rumors about them both. Then one day, Hester came back to live alone in her old cottage. No one ever knew for certain what happened to Pearl, but it was believed that she was married and had children of her own. Although Pearl would probably have been happy to have her mother live with her, Hester's real home was there in her cottage in her old town. Hester became a respected woman to whom the younger women of the community would go to for advice. Eventually, Hester dies and is buried close to Dimmesdale's grave. Her headstone reads: "On a field, sable, the letter A gules." Which means "a red coat of arms on a shield with a black background"; in other words, Hawthorne may be saying that what was once a letter of shame had now become a family's coat of arms—a badge of honor marking the woman who eventually pulled herself from shame to glory.

Symbolism

The Scarlet Letter

The letter A that Hester wears throughout the novel is not only a letter that stands for the sin that she committed, but also expresses who she is as a sinner and a woman. The letter alienates her from society and brings with it a life of loneliness. The letter becomes her identity and she learns to accept everything that comes with it, including the staring eyes of the town every time she goes to the market-place. The letter is a symbol for punishment and penance in general, and a reminder to all those who look at it of the consequences of their actions. As Hester becomes more comfortable with the token on her breast, she also becomes acutely aware of the sins of those around her. As she looks into the eyes of the citizens she can see their guilt, and as she walks by certain people she can feel the power of their goodness or the severity of their sins. The letter becomes a type of radar to Hester that gives her some comfort knowing that she has sinning companions around her.

As time goes on, the letter becomes more and more adorned with embroidery, and after awhile even changes in meaning. The townspeople gradually forget that the A stands for "Adultery," and take on the belief that it stands for "Able," as Hester has proven to be a good woman who can thrive on her own and contribute to society. When the Indians set their eyes on the letter on Election Day, they believe that it could be a badge that distinguishes her as a person of high dignity. The fact that the letter has so many possible meanings simply goes to show that its meaning is in the eye of the beholder.

A Rosebush

Hawthorne mentions the rosebush which grows in front of the prison. The rosebush symbolizes nature and the ability to live despite man, since it has grown and flourished in such a hostile environment. The rosebush symbolizes both Hester and Pearl, who prove that they too can thrive and flourish despite the hostile environment in which they live. Throughout the novel, Hawthorne often compares Pearl with the natural world around her, and she is often dressed in such rich garments and colors (red) that she stands out in a world of gloomy and somber colors, as does the rosebush in front of the prison door. Upon first meeting the Governor, the idea of a red rose is also mentioned. "Pearl?—Ruby, rather—or Coral!—or Red Rose, at the very least, judging from thy hue." Hawthorne strives to convey that the consequence of Hester and Dimmesdale's love is natural and not something sinful. Perhaps, by making Pearl a manifestation of their love, he wished to say that she was a perfectly natural occurrence and not a vile reminder of sin, but a beautiful product of a true act of love.

Pearl

It is mentioned that Pearl's name was not picked arbitrarily. "Her Pearl!—For so had Hester called her; not as a name expressive of her aspect, which had nothing of the calm, white, unimpassioned luster that would be indicated by the comparison. But she named the infant 'Pearl' as being of great price—purchased with all she had—her mother's only treasure!" Pearl and the scarlet letter can be interchangeable symbols. Just as she is the physical representation of the badge that Hester wears on her bosom, so is the letter a symbol of Pearl, changing and maturing as Pearl does. Pearl is also the manifestation of a love that is true, and is also the reason that Hester pulls herself together and goes on living despite the ridicule she faces daily. She is the embodiment of the passion and spirit that brought her parents together in the first place. She also represents the beauty and natural aspects of the world, especially in the Puritan world that can be so strict and somber.

The Scaffold

The scaffold is a symbol of Puritanism and punishment, as well as of penance. The scaffold can also symbolize the Judgment Day of God, as it is the place where the citizens are judged and oftentimes serve their punishment. The scaffold and the idea of public humiliation is very typically Puritan, reminding all those who walk by the scaffold of the punishment that awaits them if they sin. In this way it serves to keep people in line with a very strict moral code.

The Meteor
This meteor which flashed the letter A in the night sky shows that symbols can often be arbitrary and ambiguous. Citizens take the flash of A to mean "angel," since Governor Winthrop died that evening. However, Dimmesdale feels it is a symbol of his own sin and a sign that he should be sharing Hester's punishment. For Dimmesdale, the meteor is deeply significant and a reminder of his sin, which he cannot escape. For the citizens, the meteor also has significance, but in a completely opposite way. The belief in the sighting also shows the Puritan's belief in superstition and the supernatural.

The Forest
Many times in the novel, Dimmesdale retreats to the forest to find peace and solitude, although he is unknowingly accompanied by Chillingworth. For the most part, the forest is a symbol of freedom and escape. The Indians who live in the wilderness are free from the strict rule and oppressions of the Puritan society. Also, only in the forest can Hester and Dimmesdale freely express how they feel and are free to make plans for their future together. Only in the forest can Hester take off her badge and let down her hair, the weight of the burden of sin lifted. Ironically, however, the forest also represents sin and evil. The Black Man is believed to dwell in the forest, and the Indians, who are viewed as evil savages, also live there. The forest represents the unknown—the wild, and uninhibited—which is viewed as an escape from the strict moral and ethical boundaries of the Puritan church.

Themes

Identity
Throughout the novel, each of the main characters struggle with their identities. Hester is constantly growing and changing, and realizes and accepts the consequences of her actions. She matures and grows into a woman who tries to raise her child to the best of her ability, and eventually becomes a respected woman in the community. She does not hide who she is or what she has done, but still strives to find her identity despite her crime and subsequent public humiliation.

Dimmesdale has perhaps the most difficult struggle with his identity in the novel because he must hide who he truly is and how he really feels because of his stature in the community. Many times he wants to run into the middle of the street and shout the truth about his life, but his reverence and love for his community keep him from doing so. He is pulled by two different forces—his parishioners and his love for Hester—to be two different men. He feels like a fraud to his community and like pollution to their religious lives. As the novel proceeds, this inner struggle takes physical form and he becomes emaciated and ill. He finds peace at the end of his life when he confesses the truth on the scaffold and stands unified with Hester and Pearl.

The one character who willingly hides who he is, Chillingworth, takes on a new identity to exact revenge. He makes Hester promise to keep his secret and takes on the new identity of a doctor so that he can get close to Dimmesdale. He becomes a parasite who can only live while he is leeching on another person's misery. No one ever finds out that he used to be Hester's husband and a scholar in England. In the end, Chillingworth dies because after Dimmesdale confesses his sin, he has no purpose or goal in life.

Finally, even Pearl asks her mother who she is and where she came from, seeking her elusive identity. Time and time again Hester answers Pearl that she comes from God, but this answer does not pacify the child. Many times Hester wonders if Pearl is not the work of the devil, brought to her to torment her for her sin, and often refers to her as an elf or imp-child. Not until Pearl kisses her father on the scaffold does Pearl seem to come to peace about who she is, as is evident by the rumor that she goes on to live a perfectly normal life with a husband and children of her own.

The Nature of Evil

Hawthorne revisits this theme throughout the novel through various devices, such as the characters Mistress Hibbins and Roger Chillingworth, the mention of the Black Man, and the psychological effects of sin, as Dimmesdale experiences.

Mistress Hibbins often talks about being acquainted with the Black Man, the devil, and often offers to Hester to go with her into the forest to meet him. When Dimmesdale comes out of the forest after his meeting with Hester, he comes across Mistress Hibbins, who knows where he has been and associates the look in his eyes with being under the influence of the devil. Mistress Hibbins becomes the embodiment and voice of evil and the devil, tempting them to join him in sin.

Roger Chillingworth is another embodiment of evil. His desire to destroy another person makes him the antithesis of good in every way. He uses all his powers and energy to wrench the life out of Dimmesdale and in doing so, also ruin Hester's life.

The fear of the devil was such a powerful force in Puritan society that it became personified in the form of a forest entity know as the Black Man. The mention of the Black Man comes up often throughout the novel. As a presence that cannot be seen or spoken to, the Black Man is the nature of evil in the form of temptation in the daily lives of the townspeople. Whether it came in the form of adultery, theft, or gossip depended on each person's temptation.

Finally, there is the nature of evil through sin. Dimmesdale is the perfect example of evil taking root in the body of a person and infecting the soul. Although Dimmesdale repented his action, the guilt of his sin was still alive in his heart and it consumed him to the point of death. The devil and his temptation lived on with Dimmesdale long after the act was committed, and was eventually what destroyed him.

The Human Condition

One of the major acclaims of this novel was the focus that Hawthorne brought to the human condition. Throughout the story, the reader has insight into Hester's loneliness and isolation, Dimmesdale's torment, and Chillingworth's evil thirst for revenge. The reader sees into the characters in a way that evokes compassion or contempt. Hawthorne questions the value of human life in such a strict and unyielding society and provokes thought about what might really be going on with those who inhabit such a society. The narrative voice lets the reader explore the feelings of isolation and embarrassment that Hester faced as she stood on the scaffold or walked through the market-place. The anguish that Dimmesdale faced brought to light the beauty of honesty and self-truth. Even the hate that Chillingworth felt allowed the reader to see into the mind of a person who has nothing to live for or who lives only to harm others.

Sin, Guilt, and Shame

The novel examines how each of the characters deals with sin, guilt, and shame in their own way. Hester faces her sin, is found guilty, and is therefore put to shame. She knows what she has done and does not hide from it. She accepts her new life under the stigma of the scarlet letter and eventually lives a fruitful life in which she is respected. Dimmesdale, on the other hand, cannot come to terms with his sin and his guilt eats him alive. He cannot convince himself that the sin he and Hester committed was out of pure love. He feels shame every time he is commended by one of his parishioners and feels that he is being deceptive to his community and a hypocrite every time he gives a sermon. Chillingworth, as opposed to the other characters, feels no guilt or shame for his sins. He simply sees his actions as a means to an end and does not feel that he should repent. His cold and inhuman attitude toward Dimmesdale's suffering proves the evil root of his character and his inability to be saved from eternal punishment.

Pre-Reading Ideas and Activities
Suggested activities prior to the study of *The Scarlet Letter:*

1. Have students read Cotton Mather's "The Trial of Bridget Bishop" from *The Wonders of the Invisible World* by Cotton Mather (1692).
2. Have students read John Winthrop's "A Trial for Adultery" from *The History of New England from 1630 to 1649* by John Winthrop (1853).
3. Have students journal/discuss the following quote by Socrates: "The unexamined life is not worth living."
4. Have students journal/discuss the following quote by John Dryden: "Love is love's reward."
5. Have students journal/discuss the following quote by Fredrick II: "Religion is the idol of the mob; it adores everything it does not understand."
6. Have students journal/discuss the following quote by Stephen King: "The beauty of religious mania is that it has the power to explain everything. Once God (or Satan) is accepted as the first cause of everything which happens in the mortal world, nothing is left to chance...logic can be happily tossed out the window."
7. Have students journal/discuss the following quote by Anne Frank: "Laziness may appear attractive, but work gives satisfaction."
8. Have students journal/discuss the following quote by Thomas Szasz: "Punishment is now unfashionable...because it creates moral distinctions among men, which, to the democratic mind, are odious. We prefer a meaningless collective guilt to a meaningful individual responsibly."
9. Have students journal/discuss the following quote by Margaret of Navarre: "Man is wise...when he recognizes no greater enemy than himself."
10. Have students journal/discuss the following quote by Henrick Ibsen: "The strongest man in the world is he who stands most alone."
11. Have the student's journal: "One time when I felt lonely was..." or "One time when I felt unwanted or cast aside was..." This will get the students thinking about Hester's state of mind throughout the novel.
12. As a social experiment, have students cut out the letter A from a piece of red paper or felt and embellish it and wear it on their chests for a day (or week) and take note of how other people react. Also have students log their feelings about the way they are looked at or treated. Discuss the results in class.
13. Ask students to do their own research on Puritan life and the history of Puritan origins in England.
14. Have students watch *The Scarlet Letter* movie and write a review. Later, have them compare the movie to the book. (Research different versions of *The Scarlet Letter* before you decide which one you want the students to watch. Some versions closely follow the novel while others do not.)
15. Have students read the short description/summary of *The Scarlet Letter* that is found on the back cover of the book. From the information on the back cover, have them write an original short story about what they think will happen in the novel. They should include information and plot points about any of the names from the back cover and make sure that their stories have a beginning, middle, and end.
16. Have students look up all of the vocabulary words and use each one in an original sentence.

Post-Reading Extension Activities and Alternative Assessment

Cross-Curricular Activities (Multiple Subjects)

1. Create a poster about the life and works of Nathaniel Hawthorne. The poster should include dates, all his major works, important events in his life, and how his life influenced his work.
2. Pretend you are the casting director of the next *The Scarlet Letter* movie to be produced. Choose modern day actors, or even famous actors of old movies to cast in this new film. Create a poster with a picture of each actor and the character they will be playing. Also, on the back of the poster, write a short explanation of why you chose each actor for that specific role.
3. Create a poster or PowerPoint presentation of the different forms of punishment the Puritans used. Explain each method and why they might have chosen that specific punishment for that particular crime. The project should include pictures and clear identification of each form of punishment.
4. Create a newspaper of the day Arthur Dimmesdale confessed his sin and died in front of the whole town. Include as many details of the event as possible in the main article. Also include other newsworthy events, advertisements, and interesting columns (gossip, horoscope, advice, obituaries) that you might find in any newspaper to enhance the project. Make sure your newspaper has a catchy title and headlines that will grab a reader's attention, and try to include pictures or drawings when they seem appropriate. Use newsprint if possible. Try to write your articles in the same *tone* as the novel.
5. Create and decorate a scarlet letter of your own. From a piece of construction paper, draw the letter A and then decorate it so that it represents you. You can use whatever decoration or materials you want, as long as it represents your personality and beliefs. After decorating your own scarlet letter, cut it out and wear it on your chest for 1 or 2 days at school. Pay attention to the reaction you get from people who look at you and notice the letter. Does anyone act differently or say anything out of the ordinary? Keep track of your observations; after reviewing your notes, write a short paper about what you observed and how you felt while wearing the letter.

Science/Technology

6. Create a PowerPoint presentation about the beliefs of the Puritans. Include at least 10 slides, each with some type of summary or brief explanation of the topic and at least one picture per slide.
7. Use a publishing program to create a brochure about the lives of Puritans in early America. Include information about their daily lives, recreation, work, family life, etc. Be sure to include clip art or other pictures in your brochure.

Art/Music

8. Pretend that you are Hester Prynne and you are watching your daughter Pearl grow up. Create a scrapbook that chronicles the important or special events in Pearl's life, such as her birth, her christening, her first tooth, her wedding, her first child, etc....The scrapbook should include at least 8 entries and should include pictures, writing, and even decorations. Try to make it as realistic as possible, using events from her early life as a basis.
9. Make an illustrated timeline of the events in *The Scarlet Letter*. Include all of the important events in chronological order (from first to last) and also include an illustration which represents each event. Your timeline should include no less than eight important events.
10. Create a poster that details at least two or three of the major themes of the novel. Include key words and examples that support the theme and pictures or drawings that help illustrate the theme.

Social Science/History

11. Complete a simple Venn Diagram as a class or individually to connect the importance of the historical context with that of Nathaniel Hawthorne's biography to see how each influenced the novel. On one side, explore Nathaniel Hawthorne's biography. Use the biography on page 10 or research further for more information on Hawthorne. On the other side, research Puritan life, beliefs, and punishments either through the Historical Context reading on pages 12-14, or further research. Once you have your information, find the similarities between the two, noting how these two elements came together in *The Scarlet Letter*.
12. Create an informative poster about the Puritan way of life and their beliefs. Include important information about the history of the Puritans and the English church, Puritans in America, and daily Puritan life. The poster should include information in bullet form and plenty of pictures.

Essay/Writing Ideas

Essay Ideas

1. Compare and contrast the characters of Dimmesdale and Chillingworth. Consider their personalities, motivations, and relationships. How are they alike and how are they different? How do their personalities, beliefs, and motivations spur them in different or similar directions?

2. Compare and contrast the characters of Hester and Dimmesdale. Consider their situations and how they each handle the pressure's they are under. How are they alike and how are they different? What do they have in common and what sets them apart?

3. Compare and contrast Mistress Hibbins and Chillingworth. Consider their propensity for dabbling with the devil. How are they alike and how are they different? Between the two characters, which do you believe is the greater evil? Why?

4. Write a full character analysis of Hester, Pearl, Dimmesdale, and Chillingworth. Analyze their motivations, actions, personalities, relationships, and even their desires. Then draw a picture of what you think each character might have looked like.

5. Pick one theme from the novel and prove that it is the major theme of the work. Make sure that you use examples and quotations from the novel to prove your point.

Writing Ideas

6. Although in the 1600's Puritan society the justice system was very different from today. It does not seem that Hester received a fair trial or was even able to properly defend herself. What do you think are some reasons this might have happened? Is this perhaps a result of her being a woman, or simply because this is the society she chose to belong to? Also, if this story took place in more modern times, how might the justice system have worked differently for Hester? How might a lawyer have defended Hester?

7. Over the seven years that the novel takes place, it seems as though Hester and Dimmesdale hardly have any contact at all. But what if they were secretly writing love letters to one another? What might they say and sound like? Write at least 4 love letters from each of the lovers (totaling 8) in Old English as used in the novel.

8. How might the story have changed if it had been told from Pearl's point of view? How would the narration be different? How would the feel and tone of the story be different? Choose three scenes from the novel and briefly rewrite them from Pearl's point of view.

9. Compare and contrast the movie and the book version of *The Scarlet Letter*. How are they alike and how are they different? Which version do you like better? Why? Do you think the casting was appropriate? If not, how would you change it? (See #14, page 105.)

10. The ending of this novel is not exactly considered "happily ever after." Write an alternative ending, whether a happy ending or not, to *The Scarlet Letter*. What might have happened if Dimmesdale hadn't confessed? What would have happened if Dimmesdale hadn't died? What if Hester, Dimmesdale, and Pearl actually made it to Bristol without Chillingworth?

11. Write a "lost" chapter or scene from this book. Make sure to include exactly where you think it fits in. Also, be specific about the location, the time, the characters, the dialogue, and be as descriptive as possible. Try to write in the style of the author. After writing the scene, include a paragraph or two which explain how you feel this scene would contribute to the novel.

12. Conduct an interview with one of the characters from the novel. This interview could be the character's chance to explain their motivations and actions. Write and answer at least 10 questions that will give the character a chance to tell his or her side of the story. Be sure the questions are answered "in character."

13. Write an obituary for Arthur Dimmesdale. Make sure to include the major accomplishments in his life, what family he left behind, how he died, and when and where the funeral services will be held.

14. Write an obituary for Hester Prynne. Make sure to include the major accomplishments in her life, what family she left behind, how she died, and when and where the funeral services will be held.

15. What might Hester Prynne's diary/journal look like? Pretend you are Hester and create a diary of your own. Include at least 12 entries in the diary that realistically convey the feelings and experiences Hester might have gone through over the course of the novel.

16. What might Roger Chillingworth's diary/journal look like? Pretend you are Chillingworth and create a journal of your own. Include at least 12 entries in the journal that realistically convey the feelings and experiences that Chillingworth might have gone through over the course of the novel.

Project Rubric A

Category	Score of 4	Score of 3	Score of 2	Score of 1	Score of 0	Score
Required Elements	Includes all of the required elements as stated in the directions.	Includes all but one or two of the required elements as stated in the directions.	Missing 3 or 4 of the required elements as stated in the directions.	Missing 5 or 6 of the required elements as stated in the directions.	Project does not follow the directions.	
Graphics, Pictures	All pictures, drawings, or graphics are appropriate, and add to the enjoyment of the project.	Some pictures, drawings, or graphics are included, are appropriate, and add to the enjoyment of the project.	A few pictures, drawings, or graphics are included and are appropriate to the project.	A few pictures, drawings, or graphics are included, but may not be appropriate to the project, or may be distracting.	No pictures or drawings are used and/or if used are inappropriate or distracting to the project.	
Creativity	Exceptionally clever and unique; design and presentation enhance the project.	Clever at times; thoughtfully and uniquely presented.	A few original or clever touches enhance the project.	Little evidence of uniqueness, individuality, and/or effort.	No evidence of creativity or effort. Project is not unique.	
Neatness, Appeal	Exceptionally neat and attractive; typed or very neatly hand-written, appropriate use of color, particularly neat in design and layout.	Neat and attractive; typed or neatly handwritten, good use of color, good design and layout.	Generally neat and attractive; handwritten, some use of color, some problems in design and layout.	Distractingly messy or disorganized; handwritten; little use of color; several problems in design and layout.	Work shows no pride or effort. Project is incomplete, illegible, or particularly messy and unattractive.	
Grammar, Spelling, Mechanics	Little or no problems with grammar, spelling, and/or mechanics. Project was clearly proofread.	A few problems with grammar, spelling, and/or mechanics. Errors are minor and do not distract from the project.	Several errors in grammar, spelling, and/or mechanics. Errors can be slightly distracting at times.	Several problems with grammar, spelling, and/or mechanics. Errors are distracting.	Many problems with grammar, spelling, and/or mechanics. Mistakes clearly show project was not proofread.	

Comments:

Final Score: _____ out of 20

Project Rubric B

Category	Score of 4	Score of 3	Score of 2	Score of 1	Score of 0	Score
Required Elements	Includes all of the required elements as stated in the directions.	Includes all but one or two of the required elements as stated in the directions.	Missing 3 or 4 of the required elements as stated in the directions.	Missing 5 or 6 of the required elements as stated in the directions.	Project does not follow the directions.	
Creativity	Exceptionally clever and unique; design and presentation enhance the project.	Clever at times; thoughtfully and uniquely presented.	A few original or clever touches enhance the project.	Little evidence of uniqueness, individuality, and/or effort.	No evidence of creativity or effort. Project is not unique.	
Neatness, Appeal	Exceptionally neat and attractive; typed or very neatly hand-written, appropriate use of color, particularly neat in design and layout.	Neat and attractive; typed or neatly handwritten, good use of color, good design and layout.	Generally neat and attractive; handwritten, some use of color, some problems in design and layout.	Distractingly messy or disorganized; handwritten; little use of color; several problems in design and layout.	Work shows no pride or effort. Project is incomplete, illegible, or particularly messy and unattractive.	
Grammar, Spelling, Mechanics	Little or no problems with grammar, spelling, and/or mechanics. Project was clearly proofread.	A few problems with grammar, spelling, and/or mechanics. Errors are minor and do not distract from the project.	Several errors in grammar, spelling, and/or mechanics. Errors can be slightly distracting at times.	Several problems with grammar, spelling, and/or mechanics. Errors are distracting.	Many problems with grammar, spelling, and/or mechanics. Mistakes clearly show project was not proofread.	
Citation of Sources	All graphics, pictures, and written work are original, or if they have been obtained from an outside source, have been properly cited.	All graphics, pictures, and written work that are not original or have been obtained from an outside source have been cited, with a few problems.	All graphics, pictures, and written work that are not original or have been obtained from an outside source have been cited, with several problems.	Some attempt has been made to give credit for unoriginal graphics, pictures, and written work.	No attempt has been made to give credit for unoriginal graphics, pictures, and written work.	

Comments:

Final Score: _____ **out of 20**

Response to Literature Rubric
Adapted from the **California Writing Assessment Rubric**
California Department of Education, Standards and Assessment Division

Score of 4

- ❑ Clearly addresses all parts of the writing task.
- ❑ Provides a meaningful thesis and thoughtfully supports the thesis and main ideas with facts, details, and/or explanations.
- ❑ Maintains a consistent tone and focus and a clear sense of purpose and audience.
- ❑ Illustrates control in organization, including effective use of transitions.
- ❑ Provides a variety of sentence types and uses precise, descriptive language.
- ❑ Contains few, if any, errors in the conventions of the English language (grammar, punctuation, capitalization, spelling). These errors do not interfere with the reader's understanding of the writing.
- ❑ Demonstrates a *clear* understanding of the ambiguities, nuances, and complexities of the text.
- ❑ Develops interpretations that demonstrate a thoughtful, comprehensive, insightful grasp of the text, and supports these judgments with specific references to various text.
- ❑ Draws well supported inferences about the effects of a literary work on its audience.
- ❑ Provides *specific* textual examples and/or personal knowledge and details to support the interpretations and inferences.

Score of 3

- ❑ Addresses all parts of the writing task.
- ❑ Provides a thesis and supports the thesis and main ideas with mostly relevant facts, details, and/ or explanations.
- ❑ Maintains a generally consistent tone and focus and a general sense of purpose and audience.
- ❑ Illustrates control in organization, including *some* use of transitions.
- ❑ Includes a variety of sentence types and *some* descriptive language.
- ❑ Contains some errors in the conventions of the English language. These errors do not interfere with the reader's understanding of the writing.
- ❑ Develops interpretations that demonstrate a comprehensive grasp of the text and supports these interpretations with references to various text.
- ❑ Draws supported inferences about the effects of a literary work on its audience.
- ❑ Supports judgments with some specific references to various text and/or personal knowledge.
- ❑ Provides textual examples and details to support the interpretations.

Score of 2

- ❑ Addresses *only parts* of the writing task.
- ❑ S*uggests* a central idea with *limited* facts, details, and/or explanations.
- ❑ Demonstrates *little* understanding of purpose and audience.
- ❑ Maintains an *inconsistent* point of view, focus, and/or organizational structure which may include *ineffective or awkward* transitions that do not unify important ideas.
- ❑ Includes *little* variety in sentence types.
- ❑ Contains *several errors* in the conventions of the English language. These errors may interfere with the reader's understanding of the writing.
- ❑ Develops interpretations that demonstrate a limited grasp of the text.
- ❑ Includes interpretations that *lack* accuracy or coherence as related to ideas, premises, or images from the literary work.
- ❑ Draws *few* inferences about the effects of a literary work on its audience.
- ❑ Supports judgments with *few, if any,* references to various text and/or personal knowledge.

Score of 1

- ❑ Addresses *only one part* of the writing task.
- ❑ *Lacks* a thesis or central idea but may contain *marginally related* facts, details, and/or explanations.
- ❑ Demonstrates *no* understanding of purpose and audience.
- ❑ *Lacks* a clear point of view, focus, organizational structure, and transitions that unify important ideas.
- ❑ Includes *no* sentence variety; sentences are simple.
- ❑ Contains *serious errors* in the conventions of the English language. These errors interfere with the reader's understanding of the writing.
- ❑ Develops interpretations that demonstrate *little* grasp of the text.
- ❑ *Lacks* an interpretation or *may* be a simple retelling of the text.
- ❑ *Lacks* inferences about the effects of a literary work on its audience.
- ❑ *Fails* to support judgments with references to various text and/or personal knowledge.
- ❑ *Lacks* textual examples and details.

Vocabulary with Definitions

Chapters 1-3

1. beadle: noun; a minor church official who ushers or helps preserve order during services
2. contumely: noun; insulting display of contempt in word or action; a humiliating insult
3. ignominy: noun; total loss of dignity; disgrace; shame
4. inauspicious: adj.; unfavorable; boding ill
5. mien: noun; a person's general appearance or carriage; often indicates a person's mood or state of mind
6. physiognomies: noun; faces; the outward appearance of things
7. pillory :noun; a wooden framework with holes for securing the head and hands, designed to expose a criminal to public ridicule or abuse
8. remonstrance: noun; an argument in protest of; complaint; objection
9. sagacity: noun; wisdom; profound knowledge and insight to the world
10. vie: verb; to compete; to struggle for dominance or control

Chapters 4-6

1. anathemas: noun; curses; denunciations; bad wishes
2. draught: noun; a drink; a dose; that which is taken in by drinking or inhaling
3. efficacy: noun; effectiveness; capacity for producing effects
4. expostulation: noun; complaint; earnest protest
5. gesticulation: noun; an animated or exercised gesture; gestures made in an excited manner especially with or instead of speech
6. paramour: noun; illicit lover; a beloved person
7. phantasmagoric: adj.; displaying an optical illusion; imagining changing scenes
8. quaff: verb; to drink heartily
9. sable: adj. or noun; dark and somber; mourning garments
10. uncongenial: adj.; disagreeable; not compatible; not pleasing; not well-suited

Chapters 7-9

1. cabalistic: adj.; mystic; occult
2. chirurgical: adj.; surgical
3. contagion: noun; the ready transmission or spread, as of an attitude, idea, or emotion from person to person; harmful or undesirable contact or influence
4. deportment: noun; demeanor; conduct; behavior
5. despondent: adj.; dispirited; feeling or showing profound hopelessness; discouraged
6. emaciated: adj.; gradually wasted away; abnormally thin, marked by lack of nutrition or disease
7. erudition: noun; knowledge acquired by study or research; learning; scholarship
8. imperious: adj.; dictatorial; urgent; commanding
9. leech: noun; a person who clings to another for personal gain; parasite; also a name for a doctor in the 1600's; verb; to cling and to feed upon so as to drain
10. pestilence: noun; a deadly epidemic disease; something harmful or evil

Chapters 10-12

1. demerits: noun; punishments for wrongdoing
2. ethereal: adj.; light or airy; tenuous; extremely delicate or refined
3. expiation: noun; the means by which atonement or reparation is made
4. inextricable: adj.; incapable of being disentangled, undone, loosed, or solved; hopelessly intricate, involved, or perplexing
5. inimical: adj.; harmful; hostile; unfriendly
6. ominous: adj.; foreboding; threatening; portending to evil or harm
7. portent: noun; ominous significance; an indication or omen of something momentous about to happen
8. scurrilous: adj.; insulting; offensive; vulgar; grossly or obscenely abusive
9. somnambulism: noun; sleepwalking; performing acts while asleep
10. zenith: noun; the highest point or state; culmination; the point in the sky directly above the observer

Chapters 13-15

1. asperity: noun; harshness; severity in tone; roughness
2. austerity: noun; stern coldness in appearance and manner; without excess or ornamentation
3. despotic: adj.; holding absolute power; autocratic; tyrannical
4. effluence: noun; something that flows out; emanation; outward expression
5. enigma: noun; a person of contradicting or puzzling character; riddle; problem
6. gibe: noun; mocking words; taunts
7. innate: adj.; existing in one from birth; inborn; native; originating in something; not learned
8. petulant: adj.; showing sudden impatience or irritation
9. proffered: verb; offered or proposed for one's acceptance or rejection
10. requital: noun; a return or reward for service; kindness

Chapters 16-18

1. colloquy: noun; a dialogue; conversational exchange; conference
2. consecration: noun; the act of giving sacramental character; dedication to the service and worship of God; sacredness
3. denizen: noun; an inhabitant; resident
4. dryad: noun; a deity or nymph of the woods
5. harrowed: verb; disturbed keenly or painfully; distressed the mind
6. hillock: noun; a little hill
7. loquacity: noun; talkativeness; chattiness; state of talking freely
8. meditative: adj.; contemplative; deeply thoughtful
9. transmuting: verb; transforming; changing from one form to another
10. vestige: noun; a mark, trace or visible evidence of something that is no longer present or in existence

Chapters 19-21

1. depredation: noun; the act of preying upon or plundering; robbery; ravage
2. disquietude: noun; uneasiness; the state of disturbance
3. jocularity: noun; state or quality of being facetious or joking; a funny remark
4. languor: noun; physical weakness or faintness; lack of energy; lack of spirit; sluggishness
5. obeisance: noun; a bow or curtsey; a movement of the body expressing deep respect
6. potentate: noun; one who possesses power or dominion; monarch; ruler
7. prattle: verb; to utter by chattering or babbling; to talk in a simple-minded or foolish way
8. preternatural: adj.; out of the natural or ordinary course of nature; abnormal; exceptional
9. uncouth: adj.; unmannerly; awkward; clumsy; of ungraceful appearance
10. vicissitude: noun; a change or variation in the course of something

Chapters 22-24

1. apotheosize: verb; to glorify or exalt someone or something; deify
2. audacity: noun; boldness or daring without regard for personal safety
3. contiguous: adj.; touching; in close proximity with; close by
4. erratic: adj.; eccentric; deviating from the proper or usual course in conduct or opinion
5. gait: noun; a manner of walking, stepping, or running
6. indefatigable: adj.; incapable of being tired out; not tiring
7. morion: noun; helmet worn by common soldiers in the 16th and 17th centuries
8. necromancy: noun; the art of divination through communication with the dead; witchcraft
9. pathos: noun; pity or compassion
10. repugnance: noun; strong distaste or aversion; objection; antipathy

Answer Key

Due to space constraints, answers may not be given in complete sentences, as most student answers should be.

Page 9: Comprehension Check: Novel History and Elements of the Novel

1. increase in literacy rates and ability to mass produce literature
2. stories focused on chivalric love and on the actions of knights who went on adventures and performed great deeds to impress their beloveds
3. One of the first full definitions of a novel was a story that included any number of exciting and surprising events; this changed over time. In medieval times, novels did not have a definite shape. As time progressed, novels like *Robinson Crusoe* opened up the definition of a novel and many types of stories were considered "novels." Eventually, the novel became a more formatted and definite type of story which included not just the elements of romance.
4. *Answers will vary; some possible responses are:* Gothic: *Frankenstein* by Mary Shelley; *The Castle of Otranto* by Horace Walpole; *The Picture of Dorian Gray* by Oscar Wilde; *The Strange Case of Dr. Jekyll and Mr. Hyde* by Robert Louis Stevenson; *Dracula* by Bram Stoker. Romantic: *Don Quixote by Miguel de Cervantes; The Canterbury Tales* by Geoffrey Chaucer; *Rebecca* by Daphne DuMaurier; *Jane Eyre* by Charlotte Bronte.
5. *Answers will vary.* Be sure to check for explanations.

Page 11: Comprehension Check: Author Biography

1. d. all of the above
2. c. to detach himself from the actions and reputations of his ancestors
3. b. *The Blithedale Romance*
4. a. the Salem Custom House
5. a. Una
6. d. Herman Melville
7. *Answer will vary.* Two major factors with regards to Hawthorne's family were major influences *for The Scarlet Letter.* The first is that members of his family were some of the first people to settle in "The New World" and live much like he describes in his novel. They lived a Puritan life and faced the same hardships that the people in *The Scarlet Letter* face. The other major influence was the fact that his great-grandfather was a judge who presided over the Salem Witch Trials and was therefore responsible for putting to death many Salem citizens. This troubled Hawthorne and made him question the Puritan standards and way of life.

Page 15: Comprehension Check: Historical Context

1. b. person who was part of the religious and social movement of the 1500s who called for the reformation of the Church of England
2. b. The Mayflower Compact
3. d. all of the above
4. c. the Church and God
5. a. indentured servants
6. a. vengeance and public humiliation
7. c. having to stand on the pillory for hours, usually in the stockade

Answers will vary. Sample responses are given.

8. The devil was much more than just a Biblical/religious figure to the Puritans. Because there was so much uncertainty at the time, people feared what they did not know or understand, therefore they held on much more tightly to the things they could explain. When something went beyond their realm of comfort, they immediately placed the blame on something else that could not be seen or explained—something that was much more alarming and sinister. The devil symbolized all of their fears, not just temptation or evil actions. The devil became a code word for the unknown, strange, or unexplainable. Anything that did not fit into their strictly built world was work of the devil. However, in a strictly religious context, the devil was thought of as a demon that might infect a person and cause them to commit evil acts or not have control of himself. Because the Puritans took such a strict reading and meaning of the Bible, they felt that the possibility of the devil taking over a person's body was quite probable, understandably causing great fear and anxiety.

9. What Puritan leaders feared most, aside from the devil, was dissention. They did not want anyone to deviate from the "utopian society" which they had established under the laws of God. To deviate from the norms set up by society meant that the person was deviating from the laws set forth by God, and therefore sinning. The lawmakers probably felt that if they let even one crime go unpunished it was like saying to the rest of the society "it's okay to do this," and they could not afford to let this happen. They knew that if the majority of society was not happy, they would soon have a revolution on their hands, just like the one they started in England. With punishments such as branding and public humiliation, lawmakers hoped that the severity would decrease crime and further encourage the citizens to stay on the straight and narrow.

10. Puritan daily life consisted of hard work and worship. If a family was not praying, they were working or going to school (although this was rare until grammar school became a requirement for all children). Each person had his or her role, for example: men planted and caught food, while women made candles and

clothes and cooked. In the 1600s, men who were not indentured servants were free citizens who could participate in society. However, women were no more than an extension of a man's property. Women could not own land or have any political power. They were to be modestly dressed at all times and to be subordinate to men in every way. Government and religion were one and the same in the 1600s because it was the basis on which the Puritans wanted to build their society when they left England. They wanted the religious laws to be in coordination with the political laws because they felt that God's laws were man's laws. Today, we obviously live in a very different world. Although almost everyone has to work to survive, what each person does is his or her own choice. Citizens are not as strictly interdependent on one another as they were in the 1600s. People can choose whether they want to be lawyers, writers, or city workers. Today, women are equal to men and have jobs that are just as vital and glamorous. Children's roles in society have changed dramatically. They are no longer expected to work, and in fact are banned from work until they reach a certain age. Today, all children are required to attend school until the age of 16, and are not seen as property of the man of the house as they once were. Another major change in our society is the division of government and religion. Society today believes in the freedom of religion, free from the laws that govern the nation. Each person is free to believe in whatever they choose, however all citizens of the United States are unified under the federal government, which establishes rules that everyone must abide by. Punishment is no longer a matter of vengeance but rather a matter of justice and strict laws prohibit cruelty and the forms of punishment used in the 1600s.

Pages 23-24: Prior Knowledge Assessment Activity
Part One
1. Romantic
2. Psychology; motivation
3. early American setting, or Puritan era setting, or the revealing look at early American history and society
4. settle in the New World
5. judge; Salem Witch Trials
6. Ralph Waldo Emerson, Henry David Thoreau, Longfellow, and/or Franklin Pierce
7. Salem Custom House
8. Transcendentalist; Brook Farm
9. Sophia Peabody; Transcendentalist
10. The Old Manse; Ralph Waldo Emerson
11. three; Una; Pearl
12. Herman Melville; *Moby Dick*
13. The Hillside; The Wayside
14. Franklin Pierce; U.S. Consul; England (or Europe)
15. *The Marble Faun*

Part Two
1. a person who believes and follows the religious and social movement which called for the reform of the Church of England in the 16th Century
2. the Stuarts; James; John
3. reading of the Bible; prayer; preaching
4. King James Bible, or King James Version
5. Oliver Cromwell
6. Mayflower Compact
7. government; religion; societal norms; moral codes
8. God; community (or work)
9. interdependent or intertwined; together; society/community
10. deviation; God
11. public humiliation; vengeance or revenge
12. pillory; stockade
13. Benefit of Clergy; Bible
14. (fear of) the devil
15. the devil; witchcraft; the Salem Witch Trials
16. indentured servants
17. leadership; property

Page 26: Comprehension Check: The Custom House *Answers will vary.*
1. It is important to read the introduction because it introduces the reader to the author and his style, and the background of the story. It also lends authority to the story because his ancestor lived the life of a Puritan
2. Hawthorne probably mentions his ancestors so that he can explain his family situation and explain how he would be looked upon if they were still alive. Also, by being honest and open about the history of his family, he can separate himself from them and take his own stance on important issues that they may have disagreed with.
3. Hawthorne loved to write greatly detailed description of both places and people. The introduction reveals his elaborate style and ability to recreate real characters.
4. This may have been an opportunity for Hawthorne to speak freely and plainly about the story and about the time and circumstance that brought about the writing of the story as an observer rather than a participant of the story.
5. Hawthorne tells the audience about finding the papers so that the audience is aware that a woman like Hester Prynne really did exist in some point in time and that there are previous documents which record certain events that he is trying to recreate in his own novel. By telling the audience about his findings, Hawthorne is telling us about how he came up with the idea for his novel and how he was inspired to write about this specific incident and woman.

6. *Accept all reasonable responses.*
7. He hates the new political party that is coming into office and would rather be on the losing side than on their side – which he is. He ends up having a very bad relationship with the opposing political party and gets his friends involved in the fight.

Page 27: Chapters 1-3 Active Reading Guide
Answers will vary.

Page 28: Comprehension Check: Chapters 1-3
Chapter 1
1. Hawthorne describes the prison door and the rose bush in front of it.
2. a cemetery and a prison; they needed a cemetery because people inevitably die; however, the fact that crimes will be committed and people will have to be punished is also treated as an inevitability—almost as if they built the prison as a reminder to the citizens to stay in line, and if they don't there is a place for them.
3. "...some sweet moral blossom, that may be found along the track or relieve the darkening close of a tale of human frailty and sorrow" ; *answers will vary; sample student answer*—This will be a sad story about human weaknesses, but nevertheless, there is a sweet, pleasant side to the way the story ends.

Chapter 2
1. They gather to watch Hester Prynne accept her punishment.
2. Hawthorne describes the women of the New World as "coarser" and "the beef and ale" of their native land; women became less and less refined and delicate over the generations. While the women of England (the Old World) became more delicate and "fainter," these women were country women who had to work and had tan skin, sunburned cheeks, broad shoulders, and speak in a coarse and bold manner.
3. Dimmesdale is her pastor (as far as the audience knows at this point).
4. Hester is tall with dark hair and eyes. She is dignified and graceful and is wearing the scarlet letter that has been fantastically embroidered. Although she is just getting out of prison, she is radiantly beautiful.
5. She had an affair and got pregnant, despite the fact that she MIGHT be a widow; the A stands for "adulterer."
6. They are upset that she is allowed to wear something so pretty; they want her to feel the punishment, and feel that the decorated letter is more of an adornment than a punishment; they talk of ripping it off her and replacing it with something more fitting for her punishment.
7. The scaffold is a stage or platform on which the pillory is placed. It was where people would be punished in public in the Puritan community.
8. Hester's life flashes before her; she thinks about her childhood home, her mother and father, herself as a child, and even of her husband (an older man with a misshapen figure) and their home.

Chapter 3
1. the stranger's shoulder rises higher than the other (like her husband's)
2. The stranger places his finger over his lips as if to say "Shh, be quiet."
3. The stranger tells the man that he has met many hardships by sea and land and that he has been held captive by the Indians, but that he has come here to be released.
4. the townsman tells him that Hester was the wife of a learned man who lived in Amsterdam, who tried to come to Massachusetts, sent his wife before him and stayed behind to take care of some things; he has been gone over two years and no one heard any news of the husband. He goes on to tell the stranger that since her husband may be dead, she was granted pity and was forced to wear the letter instead of being put to death for her crime.
5. young clergyman from one of the great English Universities; eloquent and full of fervor; was greatly revered by his congregation; "white, lofty and impending brow, large, brown, melancholy eyes"; a strange apprehension within him; a startled, half-frightened look; simple and childlike
6. to give the name of her fellow sinner: her lover. She refuses.
7. Dimmesdale places his hand over his heart and says "Wondrous strength and generosity of a woman's heart! She will not speak!"

Page 29: Standards Focus: Allusions
1. *Answers will vary.* Students should be graded on effort and a good attempt at answering the question, not one exact right or wrong answer.
2. The allusions about Mistress Hibbins are important because they refer to a real event, the Salem Witch Trials, and the allusions explain a little bit about her personality and why people in her community might look down on her.
3. *Answers will vary with each student's experience.* Students should be graded on effort and a good attempt at answering the question.
4. *Answers will vary depending on the books and experiences of each student.*
5. If the reader understands the allusion, it conveys a whole new level of meaning. An allusion can also serve to compare a real event to a fictitious event from the text. Pros of allusions include the fact that they connect the reader to the work of literature they are reading as well as past and future readings, and they connect the author to the reader. However, the

cons of using allusions are that the reader may not know what the author is talking about, which may further alienate the reader from the story and the author. They can also be distracting to the reader to have to think about the reference of the allusion while they are already in the context of the novel they are presently reading.

Pages 30-31: Assessment Preparation: Definitions
Sentences will vary.
1. inauspicious
   a. adjective
   b. boding ill; unfavorable
   c. Ex. It was an inauspicious day to go for a drive.
2. physiognomy
   a. noun
   b. the face or countenance; the outward appearance of something
   c. Ex. Her fierce physiognomy showed that she was a strong woman.
3. beadle
   a. noun
   b. a minor church official who ushers or helps preserve order during services
   c. Ex. The beadle cleared the way so that the funeral procession could continue forward.
4. pillory
   a. noun or verb
   b. noun: a wooden framework erected on a post, with holes for securing the hands and head, to expose to public ridicule or abuse; verb: to ridicule or punish
   c. Ex. The traitor was placed upon the pillory after giving up the name of his accomplice.
5. ignominy
   a. noun
   b. disgrace; dishonor; discredit; shame
   c. Ex. After shouting racist comments, he will live in ignominy for the rest of his life.
6. mien
   a. noun
   b. appearance; a person's general appearance or carriage
   c. Ex. He was easy to spot in a room full of pompous men because he was the only one who had a noble mien.
7. vie
   a. verb
   b. to strive in competition for; contend for superiority
   c. Ex. She vied for the opportunity to be number one in the league.
8. remonstrance
   a. noun
   b. complaint; objection; protest
   c. Ex. The child's remonstrance fell on deaf ears.

9. contumely

   a. noun
   b. insulting display of contempt in words or action, a humiliating insult
   c. Ex. The contumely she showed towards the guests wearing fur coats caused many people to leave.
10. sagacity
    a. noun
    b. wisdom; profound knowledge
    c. Ex. It is amazing that at his advanced age he still has the sagacity to make sound decisions.

Page 32: Chapters 4-6 Active Reading Guide
Answers will vary.

Page 33: Comprehension Check: Chapters 4-6
Chapter 4
1. they were not sure whether she was upset enough to hurt herself or her baby, so they wanted to keep an eye on her
2. Roger Chillingworth; Hester's estranged husband
3. He wronged Hester by marrying her and therefore attaching her to an old and ailing man while she was still in the prime of her beauty and youth. She wronged him by her adultery.
4. Chillingworth asks Hester to keep his true identity a secret. *Answers will vary*
5. Chillingworth threatens to find her lover and torture him.
6. He does not want to face the dishonor as the man who was so wronged by his wife; he wants to live and die unknown

Chapter 5
1. She chooses to face her punishment and not run away from it. Also, here is the "scene of her guilt and here should be the scene of her earthly punishment"; here, she could become a martyr; also, this is where her lover is, despite the fact that they cannot be together.
2. Hester can embroider beautifully (sewing) and she makes money by embellishing clothes for any occasion and for all class levels. Hester embroiders for all types of people: the old and the young, rich or poor, military men or clergymen.
3. They are so willing to purchase her beautiful creations and enjoy her talent, but they are not willing to treat her as a human being.
4. Hester becomes a simple woman who does not indulge in any luxuries and who only spends extra money on adorning her child. She never responds to attacks made at her and gives anything she does not need to those who do.
5. The townspeople look at her and the letter and talk badly to her, saying harsh things about who she is and what she has done. The poor people she tries to help recoil from her, and the

children in the town chase her and Pearl and call them names. She dreads the children most, since they are the cruelest. They follow her and scream ugly things at her, even though they don't know what they are yelling at her. She also dreads any new member of the community, since every time they look at her, they stare the letter further into her heart and she relives the feelings of the moments when she first wore the letter.

6. Hester can feel the sin that is in the heart of a person who looks at her scarlet letter. This gives her comfort in knowing that she is not alone in the world.

Chapter 6
1. Hester named her child Pearl because she thought of her as her only valuable treasure and that she purchased her with "all she had." Pearl was the "pearl of great price."
2. Pearl is dressed with the finest cloth and with the most elaborate embroidery that Hester can sew. The text says that her mother dressed her in this way as a "morbid purpose that may be better understood hereafter."
3. Hester wonders if Pearl was sent from Eden or if she was sent by God as a punishment for her sin as a constant reminder of it. Pearl is defiant and much like Hester was when she was Pearl's age. But Hester also fears that she must be something evil and dark because she sometimes thinks she sees an impish and malicious smile on her little face and an elfish gleam in her eyes. Pearl is unable to be punished, because nothing Hester tries is effective, no matter how severe. She begins to wonder if Pearl is human at all.
4. Pearl does not get along well with the other children and hardly ever comes into contact with them. She spends a lot of time playing by herself and in nature and rebels against the other children when she goes into town with her mother. *Answers will vary.*
5. Pearl plays with whatever she can find: a stick, rags, a flower; she has them talk to each other in different voices; she never created a friend, but only has enemies who she makes fight
6. *Answers will vary*

Page 35: Standards Focus: Characterization Activity
Quotes will vary
Hester Prynne: Dynamic; round; protagonist; pg. 49 "She had dark and abundant hair"; pg. 150 "Meeting them in the street, she never raised her head"
Pearl: Dynamic; round; neither; pg. 83 "The child could not be made amenable to rules"; pg. 98 "Pearl, seeing the rose bushes, began to cry for a red rose"
Dimmesdale: Dynamic; round; protagonist; pg. 61 "a young clergyman…He was a person of very striking aspect"; pg. 133 "They deemed the young clergyman a miracle of holiness"
Chillingworth: Static; round; antagonist; pg. 55 "He was small in stature, with a furrowed visage"; pg. 128 "The

physician advanced directly in front of his patient, laid his hand upon his bosom…"
Mistress Hibbons: Static; flat; neither; pg. 108 "her ill-omened physiognomy seemed to cast a shadow"; pg. 209 "I pray you to allow my only a fair warning and I shall be proud to bear you company"
The Townspeople: Static; flat; neither; pg. 52 "They were stern enough to look upon her death, had that been the sentence"; pg. 47 "At the very least, they should have put the brand of a hot iron on Hester Prynne's forehead."

Pages 36-37: Assessment Preparation: Word Origins *Answers for (b.) will vary*
1. a. draught b. draw; drawl c. noun; a drink; a dose; that which is taken in by drinking or inhaling
2. a. efficacy b. ineffectual; efficacious c. noun; effectiveness; capacity for serving to produce effects
3. a. quaff b. *unclear or unknown* c. verb; to drink heartily
4. a. expostulation b. exposition; expository c. noun; complaint; earnest protest
5. a. paramour b. enamor; amour (amor) c. noun; illicit lover; a beloved person
6. a. uncongenial b. genius, genital c. adj. disagreeable; not compatible; not pleasing; not well suited
7. a. sable b. sword; saber c. adj. or noun; dark and somber; mourning garments
8. a. anathemas b. *unclear or unknown* c. noun; curses; denunciations; bad wishes
9. a. phantasmagoric b. phantasm; fantasy c. adj; displaying an optical illusion; imagining changing scenes
10. a. gesticulation b. gest, gestation c. noun; an animated or exercised gesture; tomake gestures in an excited manner, esp. with or instead of speech

Page 38: Chapters 7-9 Active Reading Guide
Answers will vary.

Page 39: Comprehension Check: Chapters 7-9
Chapter 7
1. to deliver to him a pair of gloves that she embroidered and also to talk to him about rumors that she has heard about the magistrates wanting to take Pearl away from her
2. Pearl is "the scarlet letter endowed with life"
3. They encounter a group of children who want to fling mud at them; Pearl runs towards them in anger and scares them off. The children don't really even know why they hate, but have been taught by example

4. The hall is wide and long and it is lined with windows. The furniture is elegant and elaborately carved. On the table there is a large chalice and other family heirlooms. On the wall there is a row of portraits of Bellingham's ancestors. Down the hall there is a suite of mail (armor) which Bellingham had made before coming to the New World.
5. a red rose; she screams, but then sees the men coming and stops because she is curious about what is happening

Chapter 8
1. Reverend Wilson, Dimmesdale, and Chillingworth
2. Rev. Wilson asks Pearl, "Who made thee?" and Pearl answers that she was not made at all, but that she was plucked by her mother off the bush of wild roses that grows by the prison door.
3. Dimmesdale; he says that God trusted her enough to be Pearl's mother, and so should the community; he also says that Pearl is a constant reminder of Hester's sin, just like the constant of the scarlet letter
4. Bellingham decides to let Hester keep Pearl but authorities have to make sure that she is being educated properly and that she goes to school at the proper age and that Hester causes no further scandals.
5. Mistress Hibbins asks Hester if she wants to come with her into the forest to meet the Black Man, but Hester declines.

Chapter 9
1. Chillingworth becomes the town physician and surgeon.
2. His health is failing and he is becoming more and more emaciated, he places his hand over his heart in pain, is pale and weak, and his voice is melancholy.
3. to finding a cure for Dimmesdale's failing health
4. the town cemetery
5. Chillingworth's appearance is becoming more and more dark and evil. His face seems to be constantly covered in soot and smoke. There is something "ugly and evil in his face". Some people start to say that he is Satan's messenger to Dimmesdale.
6. The people think that Dimmesdale is being haunted by a demon or that Satan is taking hold of him, perhaps even by way of Chillingworth.

Pages 40-42: Standards Focus: Conflict
For (c.) quotes will vary
1. a. man vs. man, external (more specifically, man vs. society)
   b. the Puritans against the Church of England; to change their idea of how they think church services should be conducted and the role God should play in everyday life
   d. subordinate
2. a. man vs. nature, external
   b. the Puritans had to endure the voyage across the dangerous waters of the Atlantic Ocean, and then had to build homes in unknown territory on harsh land
   d. subordinate
3. a. man vs. self, internal
   b. Hester struggles with feelings of guilt
   d. main
4. a. man vs. man, external
   b. one society vs. another
   d. subordinate
5. a. man vs. man, external
   b. Hester vs. Chillingworth, also, Hester vs. the community because if they find out that her husband is alive she may be put to death.
   d. main
6. a. man vs. man, external
   b. Hester needs to convince him that she is a fit mother so that she can keep Pearl
   d. subordinate
7. a. man vs. self, internal
   b. Dimmesdale struggles with his guilty conscience and often even physically punishes himself
   d. main
8. a. man vs. man, external
   b. Hester will not allow Dimmesdale to be publicly humiliated and therefore takes all of the punishment for herself
   d. main
9. a. man vs. man, external (more specifically, man vs. society)
   b. Mistress Hibbins is accused of being a witch and is therefore automatically put to death, the main punishment in Puritan society for the practice of witchcraft.
   d. subordinate
10. a. man vs. man, external
    b. Chillingworth actively works to make Dimmesdale's life miserable.
    d. Main

Pages 43-44: Assessment Preparation: Word Parts
Answers will vary according to different dictionaries.

pestilence	cabalistic	contagion	chirurgical
pest	cabal	contagious	chirurgery
destructive/ troublesome person, animal or thing	highly skilled in obscure or esoteric matters	tending to spread from one person to another	work done by using the hands; work done by hand
L. *pestilential*; plague	OFr. *cabal*; intrigue	OFr. *contagieus*; contact, infection	OFr. *cheir*; hand
-ence	-ist/ic	-ion	-ical
makes the adjective *pestilent* into a noun	makes the noun, *cabal* into an adjective	makes the adjective *contagious* into a noun	makes the noun *chirurgery* into an adjective
to destroy life or to harm	pertaining to obscure or dark matters	an infection or disease that is easily spread	a person whose work relies on their hands
Noun; a deadly epidemic or disease; something harmful or evil	Adj.; mystic; occult	Noun; harmful or undesirable contact or influence (even of ideas)	Adj.; surgical; of or by surgery

emaciated	despondent	deportment	leech	erudition
emaciate	despond	deport	leech	erudite
to waste away; diminish	to be depressed by loss of hope	to conduct or behave in a particular manner	*archaic definition:*t o cure or heal	learned or scholarly
L. *emaciatus*, wasted away	L. *despondere*to give up	L *deportare*, to carry away	OE. *lucan*, to pull out	L .*eruditus* (é- + *rud*- unformed, rough, RUDE) + *ītus* -ITE]
-ed	-ent	-ment	N/A	-tion
makes the verb *emaciate* into an adjective	makes the verb *despond* into an adjective	makes the adjective *deport* into a noun	N/A	makes the adjective *erudite* into a noun
wasted away	to be depressed or hopeless	the way one carries themselves	a person who applies leeches	knowledge; scholarship
Adj.; wasted away; abnormal thinness marked by malnutrition or disease	Adj.; dispirited; discouraged; feeling or showing profound hopelessness	Noun; demeanor, conduct, or behavior	Noun; a bloodsuck-ing creature; also, a physician (archaic)	Noun; knowledge acquired by study or research; learning; scholarship

Page 45: Chapters 10-12 Active Reading Guide
Answers will vary.

Page 46: Comprehension Check: Chapters 10-12
Chapter 10
1. They talk about guilt and secrets and confession, and Chillingworth asks Dimmesdale if he is keeping any secrets from him that may be preventing him from curing him; Dimmesdale gets upset and storms out.

2. Dimmesdale agrees that it is best for man to confess his sins, but also understands why some men might keep their sins a secret from other men. He also thinks that those who confess their sins live better than those who keep them a secret.
3. that Chillingworth is the devil
4. While Dimmesdale is sleeping, he pulls away the robes from his chest and looks at the minister's bare breast. What he sees makes him tremendously happy, although the reader is never clear what he sees.
5. *Answers will vary.* Possibly, the letter *A* carving itself on the skin over the minister's heart from the inside out.

Chapter 11
1. Chillingworth now devotes himself to torturing Dimmesdale and puts all his efforts towards making his life as horrible as possible.
2. They think he is sent from heaven as a mouth piece of God's message. They see him as a miracle and think of the ground that he walks on as holy; the fact that his parishioner's venerate him and look at him with such admiration tortures Dimmesdale and makes him feel like a hypocrite.
3. He vows to reveal himself to the public, but never has the guts to do it.
4. He is becoming more and more physically ill as his heart breaks. He is dying of a broken heart and guilt.
5. Dimmesdale hold nightly vigils in which he either stares at himself in a mirror or physically hurts himself. He whips himself and sometimes he simply sits in the dark and thinks about his sin.

Chapter 12
1. Dimmesdale goes out to the scaffold where Hester served the first part of her punishment and screams out loud without even realizing it.
2. Governor Bellingham just died, so Wilson was at the house giving last rites; Hester and Pearl were there sewing his burial gown; Chillingworth was there as his physician
3. A meteor flashes through the night sky, illuminating the sky.
4. She is mad at him and pretends to tell him, but mocks him because he would not promise to meet them at noontide tomorrow.
5. The next day, the people think that the letter *A* that flashed in the sky the night before stood for the word *angel* to represent Governor Bellingham's entrance into Heaven.

Page 47: Standards Focus: Motif
Answers will vary. Sample student answers are given

1. The Devil/Evil: References to evil and the "Black Man" in the forest plague this society. Evil is a constant threat. In Chapter 1, we learn that the prison was one of the first things built in the town; this indicates there is a constant threat over the lives of these people. In Chapter 2 we learn about Mistress Hibbons who has met with the "Black Man" and that she, herself, is evil. Mistress Hibbons even asks Hester to join her and the Black Man in the forest. This motif reveals the constant threat of evil on this society. These people truly have a fear of the Devil and are constantly afraid of being lured to the dark side.

2. Clothing: Hawthorne puts a great amount of emphasis on what Hester and Pearl wear in contrast to what the other citizens of Salem wear. In Chapter 5, a description of the ornate Scarlet Letter she wears is given. This chapter also reveals that Hester has a talent for embroidery, and it is a privilege to wear something Hester has sewn. Hester also dresses Pearl in the best clothing, either in a conscious or subconscious attempt to make Pearl (and herself) feel better about their situation. In contrast, Hawthorne also mentions the drab, colorless, and confining clothing the citizens of Salem wear. This motif reveals the irony that although Hester is supposed to be banned as an outcast of society, she is still needed for her needlework. It is also ironic that Pearl, who was supposed to be outcast with her mother, is dressed in better fineries than any child in the town. The contrast of the drab, gray clothing the citizens wear makes these citizens fade into the background of the story. Hester and Pearl, although outcast as the embodiment of sin, actually appear more special in their bright red fabric and gold thread.

3. Dimmesdale's Hand Over His Heart: Dimmesdale is in constant agony over his guilt. He feels (both literally and figuratively) as if his heart is breaking. He puts his hand to his heart not only as a reflexive action when he is feeling pain, but as shown in Chapters 2, 7, and 12, this gesture is also a non-verbal cue of his love towards Hester. It is one secret way that he can reveal his love for Hester without anyone else knowing his feelings. This motif reveals that love can actually manifest itself in physical pain. Dimmesdale deteriorates as he is struck by his guilt and inability to reveal his love for Hester.

4. Darkness and Daylight: The motif of darkness and daylight coincides with sin without punishment (darkness) and sin with punishment (daylight). One of the most important scenes takes place in Chapter 12, when Dimmesdale confesses on the scaffold. Unfortunately (or fortunately for him) there is no one there to witness his "confession." Under the cover of darkness he has finally found the strength to reveal his secret, but because it is night, there is no one

around. Had this event taken place in the daylight, he would have been publicly persecuted and humiliated for all to witness. Of course, he did not have the strength or confidence to go up on the scaffold during daylight. Similarly, the woods are considered the "darkness." As mentioned, this is where the "Black Man" dwells, and it is for this reason the citizens avoid going into the darkness of the woods at the town's edge. It is also in darkness, too, that Chillingworth tends to turn into his "evil" self, whereas during the day, he pretends to be the concerned, knowledgeable physician. In Chapter 11, after Dimmesdale falls asleep, Chillingworth even looks at Dimmesdale's chest to see his sin, where hours before, he was feigning sympathy towards Dimmesdale. This motif reveals classic night/day, evil verses good. While darkness or night is when evil occurs, daylight is when this sin is punished for all to see.

Pages 48-50: Assessment Preparation: Connotation and Denotation
Answers will vary. Sample answers are given.

1. adverse in tendency or effect; harmful; hostile; noxious/The smoke from the local brushfires is (synonym) to all of the citizens

2. marks against someone for misconduct /Josie received a (synonym) for being rude to a teacher.

3. extremely delicate; refined; light; airy/The painting with light, bright blues and whites had an (synonym) feel.

4. impossible to escape or disentangle from; perplexing; hopelessly intricate/The calculus problem the professor put on the board was (synonym).

5. atonement; amends; reparations/He made (synonym) for his crime by doing community service for the next five years.

6. the point on the celestial sphere vertically above the observer; apex; summit; highest point/As the couple stared at the (synonym) they became aware of the vast world surrounding them

7. abusive or defamatory; insulting; offensive/ Her (synonym) comments were uncalled for.

8. an indication of something about to happen; warning; omen/The black cat was a (synonym) of the luck that would befall her.

Page 51: Chapters 13-15 Active Reading Guide
Answers will vary

Page 52: Comprehension Check: Chapters 13-15

Chapter 13

1. Hester sees that Dimmesdale has become extremely weak and ill and that his moral health is taking its toll. She resolves to take matters into her own hands and do everything in her power to help him and keep him safe, even if that includes telling him about Chillingworth's true identity.
2. The townspeople think that the letter *A* on Hester's chest now stands for "Able" because she has proven herself to be a strong and capable woman, devoted to helping others.
3. Although people used to scoff at and rebuke Hester, now they are proud to have her as part of their community. The poor no longer slap away her hand and the rulers and wise men of the community no longer look at her with the same harshness as the day she first put on the letter.
4. She has become much more quiet and submissive. She is no longer as bold or as beautiful as she was the day she left jail. Her clothes are always simple and somber and her hair is always pulled back into her cap. She has completely conformed to her society.
5. *Answers will vary.* If Pearl had not come along, Hester might have indulged in the rebellious thoughts that crossed her mind and might have ended up like Mistress Hibbons, or dead. She may have dabbled in witchcraft or even done something much worse to upset the Puritan community.

Chapter 14

1. Chillingworth says that he has heard rumors that the magistrates are thinking of allowing her to take off the scarlet letter.
2. Hester says that it is not for the magistrates to decide and that if it were meant to be taken off it would fall off of its own accord.
3. Hester notices that although Chillingworth does not look much older than he is, his face is much darker, and his eyes have a red glow like fire in them. As Chillingworth becomes more and more evil and mean-spirited, his physical features reflect his internal heart. He looks more evil and dark and even surprises himself with his physical transformation.
4. Hester tells Chillingworth that she must reveal his true identity to Dimmesdale.
5. Chillingworth simply tells Hester that she may do so but that he will not stop tormenting Dimmesdale. He says that she has to do what she feels like she has to do, but that he must do the same and that he will continue treating Dimmesdale as he has been.

Chapter 15

1. Pearl plays by the shore and eventually takes some seaweed and fashions an *A* and places it over her chest to resemble the scarlet letter.
2. Pearl says that Hester wears the scarlet letter for the same reason that Dimmesdale holds his hand over his heart. Pearl realizes that her mother and the minister are connected in this way, but does not quite understand the meaning.
3. She wonders if it is time for her to tell Pearl all about the scarlet letter and about the pain in her heart and the loneliness she feels. She wonders if Pearl is mature enough to understand what she is going through.
4. Hester says she wears the *A* for the sake of its gold thread: its beauty. This is significant because it is the first time that she has lied about its meaning.
5. She feels that she is being teased and she scolds Pearl with a harshness that she has never had before.

Pages 53-54: Standards Focus: Setting

Answers will vary

1. The Prison: The prison is a symbol of Hester's new life. The mood is exciting, but scary for Hester. The reader is anxious to know what is going on and simply knowing that a crowd is standing outside of a prison says that something interesting is about to happen. The first thing the audience knows about Hester is that she is coming out of jail, although the reason is not yet told. Hester promises to keep Chillingworth's secret and therefore leaves her past behind her and starts her new life.
2. The Scaffold/Market Place: The scaffold represents acknowledgment and punishment of sin. It is the place where wrongs are settled. Dimmesdale longs to face the community while standing at the scaffold. The market place is an area with lots of movement and there are always a lot of people around, except when Dimmesdale holds his own private vigil there. Because there are always so many people and a lot of action, it creates an exciting atmosphere. It is also the place the community gathers to witness punishment.
3. The Forest: The forest is a place where truth reveals itself and where the characters can be honest and free. It creates a getaway where the characters can be themselves, free from judgment or punishment. It may symbolize freedom, hope, or truth.
4. The Governor's Hall: The hall and the mansion symbolize opulence and authority, as a contrast to the Puritan world which is centered on simplicity and austerity. The hall is decorated with family heirlooms and decadent furniture. It is an intimidating environment for Hester to be in and to make a stand for herself in front of those who judged her. Although she is afraid, she shows her strength by making her plea anyway.
5. Dimmesdale and Chillingworth's House: The house that the minister and the doctor share is

a prison for one and a sanctuary for the other. For Dimmesdale, it is where he is most tortured by Chillingworth and where he holds his introspective vigils in which he chastises himself for his hypocrisy. For Chillingworth, it is where he is most happy because he can torment Dimmesdale, while also toiling with his herbs.

Pages 55-56: Assessment Preparation: Definitions
Sentences will vary
1. gibe
   a. noun
   b. mocking words; taunts
   c. Frank made a gibe at Jane and really hurt her feelings.
2. despotic
   a. adjective
   b. holding absolute power; autocratic; tyrannical
   c. The despotic nation has finally been conquered and a democracy is replacing it.
3. austerity
   a. noun
   b. stern coldness in appearance and manner; without excess or ornamentation
   c. The austerity of her dress was appropriate for the somber occasion.
4. effluence
   a. noun
   b. the process of flowing out; outward expression; emanation
   c. The effluence with which the reverend spoke his homily inspired the congregation.
5. proffered
   a. verb
   b. offered or proposed for one's acceptance or rejection
   c. The gentleman proffered his hand to the frail, elderly woman.
6. petulant
   a. adjective
   b. showing sudden impatience or irritation
   c. The petulant child often threw temper tantrums to get her father's attention.
7. requital
   a. noun
   b. a return or reward for service; kindness
   c. Her requital was unnecessary since the Millers had given her the vase as a housewarming gift.
8. innate
   a. adjective
   b. existing in one from birth; inborn; native; originating in something, not learned
   c. Her innate aptitude for numbers was noticed even at a young age.
9. enigma
   a. noun
   b. a person of contradicting or puzzling character; riddle; problem
   c. The enigma could not be solved by even the brightest person in the class.
10. asperity
    a. noun
    b. harshness; severity of tone; roughness
    c. Her asperity was uncalled for in a situation in which the child needed comfort.

Page 57: Chapters 16-18 Active Reading Guide
Answers will vary

Page 58: Comprehension Check: Chapters 16-18
Chapter 16
1. Pearl says that the sun does not shine on her because it is afraid of the scarlet letter.
2. Pearl thinks that she will receive a scarlet letter when she comes of age; also that the letter is the Black Man's mark
3. Pearl asks if Hester will tell her a story about the Black Man; she also asks whether Hester has ever met the Black Man.
4. Hester tells Pearl that she met the Black Man once and that the scarlet letter is a mark of that encounter.
5. Pearl thinks that the Black Man set his mark upon the minister's heart when he signed the Black Man's book; she asks why he does not wear his mark on the outside of his clothes.

Chapter 17
1. Dimmesdale basically tells Hester that because his congregation loves and venerates him so much, he is more tortured because he feels like a hypocrite and therefore, more guilty. Because he cannot show who he truly is, he must suffer his guilt alone and in secret. He feels bad when people confess to him and when he looks into their eyes and knows that he himself is not being honest.
2. Hester tells Dimmesdale who Chillingworth actually is. Although he is angry at first, eventually he calms down and forgives Hester.
3. The threat of revealing Chillingworth's true identity is that now Hester may be put to death for cheating on her husband because she was not a widow when she committed adultery.
4. Hester suggests they leave Boston and go back where they came from.
5. Dimmesdale feels that life is barely worth living and that he should stay in Boston and not abandon his post or the place God has sent him.

Chapter 18
1. shame, despair, and solitude
2. Dimmesdale's sin has been kept secret and therefore he has been able to go about living his life as if nothing ever happened. He has followed the laws and rules of his society and is under the radar of suspicion.

3. Hester lets her hair out of her cap and takes the scarlet letter off of her chest.

4. After throwing off the letter, she feels like a huge weight has been lifted from her heart and it is as if her beauty floods back the moment the sunshine hits her face.

5. Pearl is at peace with nature. It is her element and she is most comfortable while interacting with it. At the end of the chapter, all the animals she encounters treat her as if she was part of their surroundings and even a wolf is curious to sniff her and let her be there without bothering her.

Pages 59-60: Standards Focus: Symbolism
Answers will vary

The Scarlet Letter	also represents *adultery* and later, *able* as the meaning changes. May also represent Hester herself, dissention from the social norms, a bold woman, or even sin in general. Ex. Ch. 2, pg. 49 "that scarlet letter, so fantastically embroidered and illuminated upon her bosom."
Pearl (and her name)	sin incarnate, rebellion, innocence, nature, beauty, or the scarlet letter itself. Pearl is the pearl of great price, and as such, Hester saw Pearl as the perfect name for her sin. Ex. Ch. 7, pg. 94 "It was the scarlet letter in another form; the scarlet letter endowed with life."
The Scaffold	punishment, truth, society, civilization Ex. Ch.2, pg. 51 "In fact, this scaffold constituted a portion of a penal machine…"
The Prison	society, civilization, law, a mental prison in each character, or even freedom Ex. Ch. 1, pg.43 "A throng of bearded men….was assembled in front of a wooden edifice, the door of which was heavily timbered with oak, and studded with iron spikes."
Roses/ Rose Bush	Pearl, life, nature, beauty, or temptation; may also symbolize the moral of the story as it states at the end of Chapter 1. Ex. Ch.7, pg. 98 "Pearl, seeing the rose-bushes, began to cry for a red rose, and would not be pacified."
hand over his heart	guilt, hypocrisy, or punishment Ex. Ch. 3, pg. 63 "Dimmesdale, who, leaning over the balcony, with his hand upon his heart, had awaited the result of his appeal."
the letter A in the night sky	superstition, omen, or sign of guilt or sin Ex. Ch. 12, pg. 152 "Not but the meteor may have shown itself at that point, burning duskily through a veil of cloud; but with no such shape as guilty imagination gave it; or, at least, with so little definiteness, that another's guilt might have seen another symbol in it."

Pages 61-62: Assessment Preparation: Word Origins
1. a. meditative   b. meditate; meditation
   c. adj.; contemplative; deeply thoughtful
2. 2. a. loquacity   b. eloquent; loquaciousness
   c. noun; talkativeness; state of talking freely

3. a. hillock   b. hill; hilly
   c. noun; a little hill
4. a. consecration   b. consecrate; sacred
   c. noun; the act of giving sacramental character; dedication to the service and worship of God; sacredness
5. a. vestige   b. vestibule, vesture
   c. noun; a mark, trace or visible evidence of something that is no longer present or in existence
6. a. colloquy   b. colloquium, colloquialism
   c. noun; a dialogue; conversational exchange; conference
7. a. harrowed   b. harrowing, harass
   c. verb; disturbed keenly or painfully; distressed the mind
8. a. transmuting   b. mutate, mutilate
   c. verb; transforming; changing from one form to another
9. a. denizen   b. inside, dedans
   c. noun; an inhabitant; a resident
10. a. dryad   b. dryadic, woods
    c. noun; a deity or nymph of the woods

Page 63: Chapters 19-21 Active Reading Guide
Answers will vary

Page 64: Comprehension Check: Chapters 19-21
Chapter 19
1. Pearl has never seen her mother with her hair loose and without the scarlet letter fastened to her chest.
2. Before Pearl comes back, she makes her mother put her hair back up and pin the scarlet letter back to her chest.
3. When Pearl comes back to her mother, she kisses her mother's cheek as well as the scarlet letter on her chest.
4. Hester tells Pearl that the minister loves them both and that someday soon they will have a home and fireside of their own; also, that she will sit on his knee and learn many things from him.
5. Pearl runs back to the brook and washes the kiss off. *Answers will vary.* She either doesn't want Dimmesdale's love, or doesn't like him, or she is unable to receive love from anyone but her mother.

Chapter 20
1. They decide that they will go back to Europe on the next boat.
2. On his way back into town, Dimmesdale is overcome with feelings of rebellion and wants to do something strange or wicked. The first person he meets is an old deacon, and while he is talking to him he has the impulse to utter blasphemous suggestions. The next person he meets is the oldest female member of his church, and normally he would recite a line of

scripture to her, but at the moment he meets her, he cannot think of any and he is not quite sure exactly what he ends up saying to her. The third person he sees is the youngest female member of his church who is pure and devout, but fearing that he may say or do something regrettable, he covers his face and pretends not to recognize her. Then as Dimmesdale passes by a group of children playing, he feels the urge to teach them bad words. *Explanations will vary*

3. When Dimmesdale runs into Mistress Hibbins she tells him that the next time he goes into the forest to meet the Black Man she will be more than happy to accompany him.
4. Dimmesdale tells Chillingworth that he no longer needs his help or his medicine.
5. rewrites his Election Day sermon

Chapter 21

1. Election Day is a celebration of the reinstating of a new governor. Some people are dressed elegantly and in different parts of the market place once might see a wrestling match or a sword fight. The gathering is followed by a procession and then a sermon.
2. Pearl asks her mother if Dimmesdale will hold both of their hands as they did by the brook the day before.
3. She realizes that at night or when no one is around, Dimmesdale freely kisses and acknowledges Hester and Pearl, but that here in the daylight and in front of the whole town, he pays no attention to them.
4. The sailor that has secured passage for Hester, Pearl, and Dimmesdale informs her that Chillingworth has also decided to join them their party and will sail with them.
5. When Hester looks up after receiving the shocking news, she sees Chillingworth staring and smiling at her.

Page 66: Standards Focus: Plot Activity
Answers will vary

Starting Action	Accept anything that includes Hester's punishment on the scaffold
Rising Action	Accept any and all actions up until the point that Dimmesdale is on the scaffold in front of the townspeople
Climax	Dimmesdale on the scaffold, realizing he can no longer hide his sin and stands with Hester and Pearl; (it should be noted that scholars also believe the climax comes in Chapter 23 at Election Day, but students have not read to that point yet.)
Falling Action	Accept anything that happens after the scaffold scene. Townspeople's reactions, what happens to the characters, including their plans to escape, Dimmesdale's "new" sermon
Dénoue-ment	Students will have to predict what happens at this point. The true denouement is that Hester comes back to her cottage; Pearl grows up; Hester dies and is buried next to Dimmesdale.

Pages 67-68: Assessment Preparation: Word Parts

preternatural	vicissitude	disquietude	uncouth
nature	vicissitude	quiet	couth
the physical world, including all natural, living things	change, of course; unexpected changes, especially a change in luck	silence; calm; tranquility	agreeable; kindly; pleasant
L. *natura* conditions of birth, natural order	L. *vicissitude* (*vice* in the place of + tude)	L. *quietus* (*qui-*, rest, quiet)	O.E. *uncuth* (un + couth)
preter-; -al	n/a	Dis-; -tude	un-
adds superlative "beyond"; changes noun "nature" to adj.	n/a	from "quiet" to "disquiet" (adj.) to "disquietude" (noun)	not couth
beyond natural occurrences; not normal	the quality of changing or turning	lack of silence	unkind; unpleasant
Adj.: abnormal; exceptional; out of the natural or ordinary course of nature	Noun: a change or variation in the course of something; alternation	Noun: the state of uneasiness or anxiety	Adj.: awkward; unmannerly; uncivil; ungraceful in appearance

potentate	obeisance	languor	jocularity	depredation
potent	obey	languor or languish	jocular	depredate
powerful; strong; effective	to submit or confirm in action	to be or to become weak or feeble	joking or jesting	to plunder or pillage
L. *potent-posse* to be able, have power power or dominion	L. *oboedire ob* + *audire* to hear	M.E. *langour* sickness; woe	L. *jocularis* equiv. to *jocul(us)* little joke	L.L. *depraedatus* plundered, pillaged
-ate	-ance	n/a or -ish	-ity	-tion
changes from adj. to a noun	changes the verb *obey* into a noun	n/a or makes the verb *languish* into a noun	Makes the adjective *jocular* into a noun	Makes the verb *depredate* into a noun
a powerful person	the act of obeying an order	the state of being weak	joking around; making fun of something	the act of plundering or pillaging
Noun: one who possesses great power; a sovereign or monarch; a ruler	Noun: a bow or curtsey; a movement of the body expressing deep respect	Noun: the state of physical weakness or faintness; lack of energy	Noun: state or quality of being facetious; joking; a funny act or remark	Noun: the act of preying upon; robbery; ravage

Page 69: Chapters 22-24 Active Reading Guide
Answers will vary

Page 70: Comprehension Check: Chapters 22-24
Chapter 22
1. On Election Day he seems completely well and recovered and full of energy. He looks as if he has never been sick and his hand no longer rests over his heart.
2. Mistress Hibbins asks Hester if Dimmesdale is the same today as he was the day before when they met in the forest. When Hester tells her that she does not know what she is talking about, Mistress Hibbins gets upset and says that she has been to the forest enough times to know who has been there by looking at them. She also mockingly asks Hester what the minister is hiding when he lays his hand over his heart. She also says to Pearl that she is rumored to be the daughter of the Prince of the Air and asks if she wants to go and visit her father.
3. Hester listens to the sermon by the foot of the scaffold where the story first began.
4. The sailor has Pearl convey the message to Hester that Chillingworth will bring Dimmesdale on board himself so that she need not worry about him.
5. Hester realizes that everyone is staring at her and the scarlet letter, as if it were the very first day she wore it.

Chapter 23
1. The townspeople think the Election Day sermon was Dimmesdale's best sermon yet and that it was more inspired and wise than any other sermon he had ever given.
2. As Dimmesdale steps out of the procession, he climbs onto the scaffold and pulls Hester and Pearl up with him where everyone can see them. He confesses his sin and reveals his chest to the crowd.
3. Chillingworth is horrified as he sees that Dimmesdale is about to die; it also seems that life is slipping away from Chillingworth as he screams "Thou hast escaped me!"
4. Before he dies, Pearl kisses her father and begins to cry and the narrator says that it is as if a spell has been broken. Pearl then becomes wholly human after acknowledging her true father.
5. The initial reaction is of awe and wonder. Just after he dies there is a great silence followed by a murmur from the crowd.

Chapter 24
1. There are many theories as to what the townspeople saw that day on the minister's chest. Some say that they saw nothing at all, while others say they saw a scarlet letter like Hester's emblazoned on his flesh. One theory says that Chillingworth produced the letter there with his magic and poisonous remedies. Another says that he inflicted the stigma on himself, while others think that it was a spontaneous representation of what was eating away at his guilty heart. However, most people do not think that there is any link at all between him and Hester and that the point of the scene he caused was a way to teach them a lesson about righteousness and holiness.
2. At Chillingworth's death, Pearl becomes the wealthiest heiress of the New World because Chillingworth leaves all of his property to her.
3. Not long after Chillingworth's death, Hester and Pearl disappear to Europe.
4. Hester comes back to her old cottage because she feels her true home is there with her former lover.
5. Since Hester returned, she has taken on the new role is that of an advisor. She counsels and comforts young women who are going through difficult times and she gives them hope for the future.
6. Most people assume that Pearl grew up to be a fine young woman who married and had a child. Proof of this comes from the trinkets that lay around Hester's house, which show that Pearl is well off and can afford to spend her money on frivolous things. Hester is also seen embroidering a baby garment which proves that Hester is a grandmother.
7. Hester is buried in a grave next to Dimmesdale, next to King's Chapel.
8. The two graves do not touch, which symbolizes that even in death, the two were not ever able to be together.

Page 71: Standards Focus: Theme
Answers will vary. Sample answers are given
1. *Repressed sin destroys the soul.*
   This was the main theme of the novel. Hawthorne was trying to prove this through Dimmesdale's pain, but was also showing that sin that is out in the open can free the soul, as in Hester's case.
   Page 63, Dimmesdale "with his hand upon his heart"
   Page 115, "thought and imagination were so active… that the bodily infirmity would be likely to have its ground works there"
   Page 133, "the agony with which this public veneration tortured him"
   Page 135, "He kept vigils"
   Page 241, Dimmesdale dies on the scaffold in Hester's arms in front of the whole town.
   Symbols/Motifs: The Black Man, Hand over the Heart
2. *Evil exists in all people.*
   This is shown through Pearl; even an innocent child seems to have reflections of evil, as her mother often comments. Chillingworth is proof that evil exists in man because he is able to torture Dimmesdale without remorse. Finally, even Dimmesdale is capable of evil, as is seen when he walks back through town after having

made plans to leave with Hester. He felt compelled to do evil and behave badly since his guilt had overcome him.

Page 89, "it was a face, fiend-like, full of smiling malice"

Page 129, "But what distinguished the physician's ecstasy from Satan's was the trait of wonder in it!"

Page 205, "at every step he was incited to do some strange, wild, wicked thing"

Symbols/Motifs: the Black Man, darkness

3. *A person's identity is partially made up by the society in which he/she lives and by those who govern it.* Hester is the main representation of this. Because of Puritanical society she lived in, she was subject to their punishments and rules, and therefore, the way she lived the rest of her life. Also, Dimmesdale shows this because as a pastor of his community, he feels the need to hide his sin so that he does not disappoint his congregation.

Page 45, "a witch, like old Mistress Hibbins…was to die upon the gallows"

Page 51, "this scaffold constituted a portion of a penal machine"

Page 92, "there was a design on the part of some of the leading inhabitants…to deprive her of her child"

Page 246, "Here had been her sin; here, her sorrow; and here was yet to be her penitence."

Symbols/Motifs: the scaffold, the scarlet letter

Pages 72-74: Assessment Preparation: Connotation and Denotation

Answers will vary. Sample answers are given.

1. contiguous—sharing a boundary or touching each other physically; adjacent, bordering, adjoining; It was difficult to focus on the professor because the walls were so thin we could hear what the lecturer in the (synonym) room was saying.

2. gait—a manner of walking, stepping, or running; walking, stepping, sauntering; Although she never said the words, Natalie's (synonym) said that she earned an A on the test.

3. necromancy—the art of divination through communication with the dead; witchcraft, conjuration, magic; The book about (synonym) had a dark cover and was bound in leather.

4. pathos—a quality or power evoking pity or compassion; pity, sadness, compassion; That piece of art evokes such (synonym) that it makes me cry whenever I look at it.

5. erratic—deviating from the proper or usual course in conduct or opinion; eccentric, wandering, queer; The (synonym) driver almost caused a few cars to drive off the freeway.

6. indefatigable—incapable of being tired out; untiring, energetic, lively; The (synonym) child continued to run around and cause havoc for another hour.

7. audacity—daring without regard for personal safety or other restrictions; boldness, temerity,

foolhardiness; The (synonym) in her tone was a warning to her husband to watch what he said next.

8. repugnance—strong aversion or distaste; objection, antipathy, reluctance; Her (synonym) for caviar was evident by the expression on her face.

9. apotheosize—to hold on a pedestal, think highly of; deify, glorify, idolize; According to the Christian Bible, to (synonym) any human is a sin.

Pages 75-76: Quiz: Chapters 1-3

1. woman in the crowd
2. Arthur Dimmesdale
3. Roger Chillingworth
4. the narrator
5. Hester Prynne
6. the narrator
7. Rev. Wilson
8. vie; verb
9. sagacity; noun
10. inauspicious; adjective
11. pillory; noun
12. contumely; noun
13. physiognomy; noun
14. beadle; noun
15. ignominy; noun
16. remonstrance; noun
17. mien; noun
18. Puritan way of life is very strict and rigid; strong rules and expectations for the citizens who live in a Puritan community. Every person has their role. Even the smallest crime is punishable by branding and/or public humiliation. Most punishments are served by being placed on the scaffold or pillory for public punishment.
19. Hester is accused of adultery and becoming pregnant by her lover, but because there is no evidence whether her husband is dead or alive, instead of being put to death, she must simply stand on the scaffold for three hours and then wear a scarlet letter on her chest for the rest of her life.
20. Hester is scarred, but strong. At times she goes within heself and thinks about her past, but at other times she is almost brought to tears by the things that people yell at her. She cannot believe what is happening to her. She decides that she and Pearl will live their lives alone and do the best they can in the community that hates and views her with disgust.

Pages 77-78: Quiz: Chapters 4-6

1. False
2. True
3. False
4. True
5. False

6. False
7. False
8. True
9. True
10. False
11. gesticulation; noun
12. uncongenial; adjective
13. anathemas; noun
14. draught; noun
15. phantasmagoric; adjective
16. efficacy; noun
17. expostulation; noun
18. quaff; verb
19. sable; noun
20. paramour; noun
21. c. "He bears no letter of infamy, wrought into his garment, as thou dost; but I shall read it in his heart."
22. b. to a small abandoned cottage on the outskirts of town
23. c. she doesn't want to leave her lover
24. d. she embroiders clothes
25. c. that she looks like a little elf

Pages 79-80: Quiz: Chapters 7-9
1. Governor Bellingham
2. magistrates (leaders); Pearl
3. she was not made at all, but plucked by her mother from the rosebush in front of the prison
4. Dimmesdale
5. Mistress Hibbins
6. chirurgical; noun or adjective
7. deportment; noun
8. pestilence; noun
9. imperious; adjective
10. erudition; noun
11. emaciated; adjective
12. cabalistic; adjective
13. despondent; adjective
14. leech; noun
15. contagion; noun
16. physician (leech); He has read a lot about medicine and the mixing of chemicals and composition of medication and remedies; he also learned a lot about the properties of herbs and roots will being held captive by the Indians.
17. They see him as a highly spiritual and educated man and they revere him. They care for him very much and they are worried about his health.
18. Some townspeople arrange for them to live together so that Chillingworth can become his personal physician and observe and take care of him at all times.
19. The window looks over the cemetery. It could be foreshadowing of Chillingworth and Dimmesdale's deaths, but also, the cemetery was symbolic of both men, as Dimmesdale was a minister and Chillingworth a physician—both who deal with the dying.

20. His face and features are becoming darker and seemingly more evil and devilish. It is as though Satan has taken over his body and is showing himself physically. He is becoming physically ugly and evil.

Pages 81-82: Quiz: Chapters 10-12
1. Chillingworth
2. Chillingworth
3. Dimmesdale
4. Chillingworth
5. Dimmesdale
6. Chillingworth
7. Dimmesdale
8. 4
9. 6
10. 7
11. 2
12. 5
13. 3
14. 8
15. 1
16. demerits; noun
17. ethereal; adjective
18. scurrilous; adjective
19. ominous; adjective
20. zenith; noun
21. inimical; adjective
22. portent; noun
23. somnambulism; noun
24. inextricable; adjective
25. expiation; noun

Pages 83-84: Quiz: Chapters 13-15
1. True
2. False
3. False
4. False
5. False
6. False
7. True
8. True
9. False
10. False
11. proffered; verb
12. requital; noun
13. despotic; adjective
14. asperity; noun
15. innate; adjective
16. effluence; noun
17. gibe; verb
18. petulant; adjective
19. austerity; noun
20. enigma; noun
21. Instead of becoming a hard and cold woman who only cares for herself and her child, she has become softer and kinder. She helps the sick and the poor. She has assimilated to her

society as much as possible. The scarlet letter helped her find her calling in life, which was to help other people with hardships.

22. Now the townspeople are proud to have Hester as part of their community, since she is such a giving person.

23. They respect her and love her and sympathize with her lot in life. They call her "Our Hester" and say that the scarlet letter stands for Able.

24. After seeing Dimmesdale on the scaffold, she is worried that Chillingworth may by starting to get the better of him and for Dimmesdale's sake it will probably be better if the two men stay as far apart as possible. She wants to give Dimmesdale a chance to detach himself from his tormentor.

25. Hester tells Pearl that she wears the scarlet letter for the sake of its gold embroidery, which is a lie. This is important because it is the first time since she received the letter that she has lied about its significance.

Pages 85-86: Quiz: Chapters 16-18
1. a. the sun is afraid of the scarlet letter
2. a. the Black Man
3. c. angry and in despair
4. d. sunshine falls upon her
5. a. like a weight has been lifted from her
6. denizen; noun
7. colloquy; noun
8. dryad; noun
9. meditative; adjective
10. hillock; noun
11. transmuting; verb
12. vestige; noun
13. loquacity; noun
14. consecration; noun
15. harrowed; verb
16. that she will receive her very own scarlet letter
17. that she met the Black Man only once, and that the scarlet letter is a mark of that meeting
18. he always holds his hand over his heart, and he is physically deteriorating
19. The more his congregants love and think highly of him, the more hypocritical he feels. He feels worse and worse about lying to them and being something that he isn't.
20. She is at one with nature. She is comfortable with it and even the animals are not threatened or annoyed by her presence. She fits right in with the animals in the forest and with the natural surroundings; nature is her best playmate.

Page 87: Quiz: Chapters 19-21
1. Dimmesdale
2. Dimmesdale
3. Hester
4. a sailor
5. Mistress Hibbins

6. the Narrator
7. Hester
8. languor; noun
9. uncouth; adjective
10. depredation; noun
11. prattle; verb
12. jocularity; noun
13. preternatural; adjective
14. potentate; noun
15. vicissitude; noun
16. obeisance; noun
17. disquietude; noun

Pages 88-89: Quiz: Chapters 22-24
1. 8
2. 5
3. 3
4. 10
5. 7
6. 2
7. 9
8. 4
9. 6
10. 1
11. necromancy; noun
12. indefatigable; adjective
13. apotheosize; verb
14. erratic; adjective
15. contiguous; adjective
16. repugnance; noun
17. gait; noun
18. pathos; noun
19. audacity; noun
20. morion; noun

21. After Dimmesdale confesses his sin, Pearl kisses him and begins to cry. The narrator states that the spell is broken; Pearl has finally received knowledge of her true father and from now on would be able to live a normal life. By showing this moment of vulnerability, Pearl has become a fully human and emotional being. From this point on, she will be able to experience life with a full range of emotion and live it to the fullest, encompassing all human experience.

22. despite the pain that she lived with while she was there, this is where her lover is and the place she considers to be her eternal home: with him and with her sin; the townspeople no longer look upon her as a scourge and she feels safe and comfortable in her old home, where she raised her daughter and lived the most important times of her life.

23. The townspeople notice that Hester is always receiving trinkets and household items that serve no purpose but to please the eyes and that can only be afforded as a luxury; Pearl, now a grown and wealthy woman, is sending

these things to her mother as tokens of affection and remembrance; Hester also embroiders baby clothes, showing that she is a grandmother

24. After Hester comes back to the cottage, she becomes a counselor to those who are suffering or facing some sort of hardship. This is important because this is something that Hester never had in her time of pain and loneliness. Also, it is important because essentially it is the same role that Hester tried to take on when she was there before through helping the poor and the sick. She is fulfilling her calling by helping others.

25. Hester is buried in a grave next to Dimmesdale's, next to King's Chapel. The two graves do not touch, which symbolizes that even in death, the two did not properly belong to each other. Although they are probably now together in eternal life, the graves symbolize their life on earth—always near each other, but never quite able to be together

Page 90-93: Final Exam
1. Pearl
2. Hester
3. Rev. Wilson
4. Chillingworth
5. Pearl
6. Hester
7. Dimmesdale
8. Mistress Hibbins
9. Pearl
10. Chillingworth
11. True
12. False
13. False
14. False
15. False
16. True
17. True
18. False
19. False
20. False
21. a. Hester Prynne
22. c. in medias res
23. a. flat
24. b. secret sin can be fatal
25. c. a New England Colony
26. d. Dimmesdale confessing his sin in front of the townspeople
27. d. both b and c
28. d. Hester is being punished for her crime
29. b. punishment
30. d. both a and b
31. d. all of the above
32. a. the main idea, or the lesson being taught in the story
33. b. the plan or main story of the novel
34. b. man vs. self

35. a. allows the reader to track the development of each character
36. *Answers will vary. Accept all answers that support the themes of the novel; answers should include evidence from the story to support the theme.*
37. *Answers will vary*
38. h. boding ill; unfavorable
39. a. wisdom; soundness of judgment
40. d. effectiveness; producing an effect
41. b. animated gestures
42. i. a deadly epidemic or disease; something evil
43. e. dispirited; feeling or showing hopelessness
44. j. demeanor; conduct; behavior
45. c. harmful; hostile; unfriendly
46. g. incapable of being disentangled; hopelessly intricate
47. f. showing sudden impatience or irritation
48. b. a person of contradicting or puzzling character; riddle
49. h. talkativeness; chattiness; state of talking freely
50. c. a dialogue; a conversational exchange
51. j. a resident or inhabitant
52. e . to utter by chattering, babbling
53. d. rude; discourteous; awkward
54. i. physical weakness; lack of energy or spirit
55. a. evoking pity or compassion
56. f. boldness or daring without regard to safety
57. g. strong distaste or aversion; objection; revulsion

Pages 94-96: Final Exam: Multiple Choice Version
1. a. Hester Prynne
2. a. the prison door
3. b. on the outskirts of the village
4. b. husband
5. a. minister
6. b. keep his identity a secret
7. a. embroidering clothes
8. d. loneliness
9. d. all of the above
10. c. flat
11. d. a and b only
12. c. elfish
13. d. Pearl
14. c. secrets can hurt one's soul
15. a. when Dimmesdale confesses his sin in front of the townspeople
16. c. torment
17. a. allows the reader to track the development of each character
18. d. "Thou hast escaped me!"
19. b. an A
20. b. in medias res
21. c. the letter A

22. d. both a and c
23. c. punishment
24. b. a New England colony
25. c. 7
26. a. the devil
27. d. both b and c
28. d. Hester is being punished for her sin
29. c. man vs. self
30. b. "Once in my life I met the Black Man. This scarlet letter is his mark."
31. b. the plan or the main story of the novel
32. a. anger and despair
33. b. kisses him
34. a. the lesson being taught by the story
35. d. "On a field, sable, the letter A gules."
36. c. pestilence
37. a. inauspicious
38. b. prattle
39. d. petulant
40. b. colloquy
41. a. languor
42. c. inextricable
43. c. pathos
44. b. efficacy
45. d. sagacity
46. a. deportment
47. c. denizen
48. b. audacity
49. d. inimical
50. b. repugnance